THESE DAYS

Edited by

Heather Killingray

First published in Great Britain in 2004 by
POETRY NOW
Remus House,
Coltsfoot Drive,
Peterborough, PE2 9JX
Telephone (01733) 898101
Fax (01733) 313524

All Rights Reserved

Copyright Contributors 2004

SB ISBN 1 84460 796 8

*F*OREWORD

Although we are a nation of poets we are accused of not reading poetry, or buying poetry books. After many years of listening to the incessant gripes of poetry publishers, I can only assume that the books they publish, in general, are books that most people do not want to read.
Poetry should not be obscure, introverted, and as cryptic as a crossword puzzle: it is the poet's duty to reach out and embrace the world.
The world owes the poet nothing and we should not be expected to dig and delve into a rambling discourse searching for some inner meaning.
The reason we write poetry (and almost all of us do) is because we want to communicate: an ideal; an idea; or a specific feeling. Poetry is as essential in communication, as a letter; a radio; a telephone, and the main criterion for selecting the poems in this anthology is very simple: they communicate.

CONTENTS

Incapable	Jillian Shields	1
Body Without Soul	Tina Rose Dolby	2
Deceit	Greta Robinson	3
Young Love	Joyce Hemsley	4
Pastures New	Christine Margaret Wicks	5
The Singles Poem	Jesamine Cook	6
Time Is A Healer	Donna Salisbury	7
The Night Monster	Aaron Tomes	8
Cold	Kate Allan	9
Lighting Time	Geof Farrar	10
We Children Of Apollo	Jonathan Pegg	11
Egypt	Patricia Adele Draper	12
Salt Bread	Peter Bauer	13
Of Whitby, Swelterpassion	Steven Ilchev	14
There Once Was A Very Cold Girl	Helen Harvey	15
Coming Of Dawn	P Brewer	16
Destiny	Jo Lodge	17
A Smile Made From Fairy Magic	C R Slater	18
Sin Holds . . .	Philip Naylor	19
The Last Goodbye	Vivienne Hudson-Lewis	20
Deliverance	Albert Russo	21
A Picnic Unique	A Jamil	22
Turbulence	Barry Woods	23
Portrait Of The Artist	S M Thompson	24
Hurtful Memories	Samantha Groves	25
The Dream	P Block	26
Sky	Ali Paterson	27
Had Enough	Mandy Jayne Moon	28
I'll Forever Love The Ones Closest To My Heart . . .	Jason Bone	29
Little Me	Robert Warren	30
Flowers Of The Spring	Nikki Biram	31
At This Time	Carole A Cleverdon	32
Money! (So What)	Susan Barker	33
The Beggar	Lorraine Cohen	34

Have A Nice Day	David M Walford	35
Outside Court No 5, Manchester	Mark A Holbrook	36
Just Grace	Joan Bennett	37
The Evolving Nap	Carla Iacovetti	38
Autumn Night	Rob Hallsworth	39
As We Leave Years Of Footprints Behind Us . . .	Stephen A Owen	40
This Generation Has No Nation	Onyeka Igwe	42
As One	Donna Davies	43
The Phoenix	Rosalind Cook	44
5 Minutes	S McKinlay	45
AMH	Barry Ryan	46
Gold	Edwin Page	47
Daughter, Witness, Gang War	Vickie Lui	48
Seascape	Tom Valentine	49
Last Whispers	Peter Elliott	50
Fond Memories	Joan Prentice	52
Noughts And Crosses	F R Smith	53
My Dreams	Marj Busby	54
I Shall Write!	High Priest	55
One-Night Stand	Alan Holdsworth	56
I Am This Dream	Richard Ward	57
The Railway Station	Mary Morley	58
Not Quite Right	Tiffany Little	59
Granny Spuds	M Illsley (Cambo)	60
They Cannot Speak	Roy Baker	61
Shadows And Reflections	Justin Lowe	62
From Mad We Came And To Mad We Return	Antonio Martorelli	63
Time To Ourselves	R N Taber	64
Feelings	Jo Seward	65
Untitled	Jayne Evans	66
Teddy	Mary Tickle	68
Untitled	Philip Allen	69
Heather	Nancy Elliott	70
What Will I Be?	Kenneth Mood	71
Dreams	Maggie Hickinbotham	72
Garden	Clare Saffell	73

Do You Want To Go To Ireland?	Geraldine McMullan Doherty	74
Really	Ellen Chambers	76
In The Desert	Clive E Oseman	77
Mountainous Triumph	Josie Lawson	78
Wedding Dress	Tina Nightingale	79
Bath Night	D E Henry	80
Mind, Body And Soul	Chris Scriven	81
Takanano	Phil Roberts	82
The Thin Red Line	Lachlan Taylor	83
Waiting	Geoffrey Matthews	84
Oh, Whatever Will Be	Dave St Clair	86
Bob Monkhouse	David A Bray	87
Vesuvio	J Cashford	88
A Dying Wish	Peter W J Baxter	90
The Widow	Norman Andrew Downie	91
A Ward Of The Moon	B Wardle	92
Wet, Wet, Wet	Lyn Sandford	93
All Souls' Day	Timothy McNeal	94
I Miss You	Keith W Hewett	95
Alice	Moira Jean Clelland	96
Lovers' Silhouette	Duncan MacFarlane	97
A Bereavement	Ellen Rowley	98
Snow Falls	James Patrick Milton	99
Our Treasure	James T Gordon	100
Unknown Universe	Gina M Clayton	101
The Vendor	Opal Innsbruk	102
Who Made Snowflakes?	Alan Pow	103
Earth To Earth	Wendy Watkin	104
An Afternoon Party	J Bradbury	105
Painting Pictures	Dennis Young	106
On You I Depend	Margaret Cameron	107
A Stranger In Line	A R Wait	108
Christmas	R Mills	110
Reality	S Longford	111
Whose Honour?	Rachel Taylor	112
Like What You See	Kara Sian Phillips	113
The Refugee	Anne Gaelan	114
The Shadow	Alan Gordon	115

Sympathy	Paul Fulton	116
And So Cold Winter	David Elsmere	117
Perpetual	Adam J Tipper	118
White Coppice	Leslie Russell Walker	119
Not Lonely But Alone	Gillian L Wise	120
Embers	John Osland	121
The Little Angel	Elizabeth Marsden	122
Tears	Mags Scorey	123
Testimony	Matt Riley	124
Safe And Secure	J Watcher-Masters	126
Matthew	Ricky N Lock	127
One True Friend	Marian Bythell	128
A Messily Starred Sky	Shuvra Rahman	129
O Muse, Ordain That I Should Sing	Malcolm Henry James	130
Self-Made Man	Brian Lunt	131
You're Not Qualified To Say That	Louise Tucker	132
The Lover's Real Answer	AnnMarie Eldon	133
About Rugby	Ali Sebastian	134
The Mystic	Colin Walsh	135
Avatar	David Randall	136
Staircase	Mary Guckian	137
The Job Seeker's Allowance	Peter Asher	138
Decisions, Decisions, Decisions	Ruth Morris	139
Subconscious Winter	Terry Lane	140
The Honesty Of You	B Lamus	141
Romney Vale	Peter Alfred Buss	142
The Rain	Ojo Idowu Opeyemi	143
Your Poem Mum	Abbie S Dixon	144
Sweet-Smelling And Warm	Steven Howe	145
A Mother's Prayer	Lillian Hutt	146
A Hole In The Clouds	Mark Musgrave	147
The Only Dance	Clive Cornwall	148
The Older Man	M C F McKinlay	149
Safe	Michael Brett	150
Daydreams	Carol Olson	151
Lovely Gran	Michael Stalker	152

Absent Mind	Thomas Allan Liddle	154
Fireworks	Jo Allen	155
Racism	Zyfe Cani	156
When The Darkness Comes	Kim Montia	157
Follow The Sun	Vicky Stevens	158
The Great Eye	Terry Ramanouski	159
The Skinniest To Win	Donna Whalley	160
Munching Maggot	Carol Ann Darling	162
People Of Third World	Ibrahim Asad	163

INCAPABLE

I am in a coffin of life,
and the lid has closed.
The red velvet feels soft but
part of me still wants to tap
and say that I am alive.
I hesitate, my fingers slide
from that hard wood of the door
and I almost lie down,
almost . . .
My ears haven't given up
trying to hear outside movement
but it stills and drops away
from the hard exterior.
There is nothing now to persuade;
all the resistance I have is memory,
colourful images of a life long passed.
Is there a point?
Will I almost sleep for eternity
or will my pendulum mind sway
in one direction?

Jillian Shields

BODY WITHOUT SOUL

He leaves me, I'm alone
and I am body without soul.

An empty glass,
a pageless book,
a life without a goal.

The time it does stand still
I feel my heart can barely beat.

And then at last he's back
and I am once again complete.

Tina Rose Dolby

DECEIT

You're laughing, life's a breeze.
You're living hard,
doing what you please.
Working long hours.
sleeping light.
Opening doors
late at night.
You can't see me.
I'm closing my eyes
for the very first time.

You're crying, miles away
in a tiny room,
hoping someone will say
it's not happening.
Shedding tears,
still making plans
for future years,
but not with me.
I'm closing my eyes
for the very last time.

Greta Robinson

YOUNG LOVE

What excitement a kiss brings
little stars glow from Heaven
now two hearts beat together
where once there was pain.

How delightful three words sound
when they're whispered sincerely
now she loves him so dearly
and his life's not in vain.

What a difference a ring makes
sparkling emeralds and diamonds
they both dance in the sunshine
where there used to be rain.

Hearken to the bells' chime
'midst the glory of young love
and with rapture beguiling
two hearts sing again.

Joyce Hemsley

PASTURES NEW
(Inspired by Angela Della Follon)

Lead me to new pastures
Meadows with primroses and bluebells
Spring in the air
Love everywhere
Find me someone who will truly care
Share my interests and my desires.

New fashions in Bakewell I will sell
Wearing my boots (puss) of soft aqua suede
Maybe move to a new dell (a)
I will search and like the cows
                graze on new land
Dance away to a lively jazz band
No longer will I be a stranger on the shore
Life will offer more and more
Perhaps one day a band of gold on my left hand.

Déjà vu, déjà vu, déjà vu.

Christine Margaret Wicks

THE SINGLES POEM

The sheets are cold and the kettle is hot.
Just me and my TV, chances, there are not!
What beats a biccy and a comfy sofa?
Other than that man, the one with the loafers!

Drifting away into Hollywood arms,
Me and my slippers, and a brunette with charms.
Microwave pings! And back to reality,
'Well that was close, nearly lost sanity!'

Meal for one and dreams for two,
The credits go up and that's my cue.
Back into bed, and the still cold sheets,
Any fantasies I have, those, I'll keep!

Jesamine Cook

TIME IS A HEALER

Time is a wonderful healer,
That's what people say.
Cures 101 ailments,
And places fears at bay.
But how long does it actually take
To get time on your side?
When is it alright to say,
'At least I tried'?
I have found that time does help,
It gives you thinking space.
It helps you back on your feet
And gives you a sense of grace.
So I'm all for supporting time,
I know how kind it can be,
I have buried all past fears
And found the real me.

Donna Salisbury

THE NIGHT MONSTERS

The night is dark, the night is cold. Someone is creeping in the
                                                      silent night.
Something red, someone mad who needs a soul to take with greed.
The devil, greedy, nasty in red-hot flames with his evil cackle
                                          dancing madly: sadly.
His hiss calls his darkest squad dancing sadly: madly.
The sun rises.
The morning bell ding-dong flashing in his face, disappearing in the
                                               morning light;
No more cackling. No more dancing sadly: madly.
The world is asleep.

Aaron Tomes (10)

COLD

Is when a death happens or when the weather outside is sombre, or when you leave your coat on the bus.
But when someone dies, it leaves a hole which is forever cold.

Kate Allan

LIGHTING TIME

Single lamp was lit all day
Torch-like mark in light of day
Renewed not when came early day
Explored surroundings night and day
Effervescent night-time and day
To single lamp his light raised time
Lamp held thoughts on how was lit
All others dark, then sometimes lit
Many with jokes, his temper lit
Pray, your jealous lamp's word's street lit.

Geof Farrar

WE CHILDREN OF APOLLO

We children of Apollo,
Children of the sun rising,
Those who set out to conquer
Our moon and the planets beyond.
The colonisers; life's survivors,
The rovers and the drovers,
The faith followers and the strong,
Those who long to find a new life,
To reconnoitre the new frontiers,
Fearlessly following their own belief.
How God said we should
Scatter our seed near and far,
To take great arks
To voyage through deep waters,
Examine endless barren fields,
Which is the great darkness of space
Overcoming hardships and adversities,
Fleeing across the cosmos,
In wondrously designed starships,
Carrying a wealth of old knowledge
From this blue and verdant planet,
This, our ancestral home,
Falling into myths and legend,
Wherever mankind settles,
Worshipping a 'Mother Earth'.
You sceptics better believe it,
For I most sincerely say,
I get down on my knees and pray
To the High One, 'I, a sun follower,
This is our true destiny; let it be.'

Jonathan Pegg

EGYPT

When we embarked on our holiday to Egypt,
Little did we know that we would find
The mysteries and grandeur of a kingdom
That flourished in the cradle of mankind.
That first morning when we woke up on The Nile
And looked from the upper deck into the mist,
We were stranded between two clouds upon the river,
Lost in time as we followed each curve and twist.
The heat was cloying even though it was early,
And the palms and dunes were shadows on the banks.
I shivered as I felt an eerie presence
And silently I murmured a prayer of thanks.
Our craft was plying waters that were ancient,
That had seen the golden Pharoah in his barge.
The Nile is the watery guardian of Egypt.
Of life and death, the river is in charge.
What a privilege it was to visit Egypt.
To live in the past with the pharaohs for a while.
Sampling sights and aromas of this mystic country,
That owes its very lifeblood to The Nile.

Patricia Adele Draper

SALT BREAD

It was an ordinary day, not too bright and not too dark,
and the lyrical quality of what might have been never was,
but that didn't matter to her.

She only wanted what millions of others desired,
not to take from them but to enjoy with them,
in a warm, liquid flow of contentment.

Her secret ambitions and open-faced joys
merely served the public avenues and that private pain,
which had revolved in cartwheels with every step of the day.

The heart she had worn on her sleeve was for the moment
trampled in the mud, stomped on and mangled
by boots retreating down their solitary path of rejection.

Carefully she unwrapped the morsel she had saved to feed
                                              her aching fears,
and in so doing unlocked a thousand tears,
a thousand years in a moment deep as night.

Salt bread for a hungry heart,
salt dreams for a sleepless head,
salt preserving hope against another wearying day of dread.

Peter Bauer

OF WHITBY, SWELTERPASSION
(To the most beautiful, effervescent, seagull lady of the Earth, with whom a sizzling early August day in magnificent Whitby was more special than imaginable)

Meet the dame of swelterpassion
swing a tear of delight
while the scintillating prism-vision
beaches are vampirically bright.
Meet the dame, breathe no longer
conventionality is thrust aside
as free-falling into magnetism
cannot be historically trite!
Whitby is within me,
my ghoulish goosebumps tell a tale
of listening to Dracula chanting
as the dame grips me
and her touch just never fails . . .
amid hot amorou-airborne sailing!
I free-fell again and again
still free-falling as I speak,
I countenance those Whitby moments
zooming forever more.
My grotesque mind will ne'er leak
ne'er again, 'tis solid now
and climbing those two hundred steps
or so to the hillways of our
kissways and that euphoric murmur:
'Oh, summergaze . . . Oh, Whitby!'

Steven Ilchev

THERE ONCE WAS A VERY COLD GIRL

There once was a very cold girl
Who thought she was going to hurl,
So she ran out of bed
Holding her head
And slipped up upon a pearl!
'Ouch,' she said, raising her head,
'At least my sickness has gone.'
For a second she thought
That she had grown a wart
And so cried for very long.
In her fright
Her hands caught alight
From the fire which burned by her side
'Oh s***,' she said, 'so has the bed,
Where shall I sleep tonight?'
Her phone then rang,
It was Gareth and Yang
Who suggested she spent her night there.
'Oh you poor soul,
You still feelin' cold?
Come to bed, it's much warmer in 'ere!'

Helen Harvey

COMING OF DAWN

Sun drifting in a cloud of red
Uncovers the moon's silky bed
Nightfall scatters darkness around
Sleepy folding leaves of flowers
Evening birds twitter none
Time to rest the sun, its work now done

Nocturnal in every form and every way
Immortal time here to stay
Ghostly, eerie, cold, chilled air
Haunting figures, everyone, everywhere
Tomorrow will soon be here

Darkness removed by sunlight rays
Amber adjusting in the dew's haze
Waking everything in its path
New day begins today to start

Today is here, yesterday gone
Imagine if sun had not shone
Measure the day to years into one
Emptiness, no new day would have begun.

P Brewer

Destiny

Our destiny is set on the day we are born
Body clock ticking down, tick, tock, tick, tock.
What will it bring this life of ours?
Will we be happy all the days of our lives?
What does this destiny of ours hold?
Destiny is what you make of it, so I am told.
Your life is in your hands so grab each day,
Live life to the full, each day so it counts.
Never take for granted, all the things that you have.
Our destiny should be to have fun in our lives.
No pain, no suffering, happiness all around,
If life was that easy, we would all know our destiny.
Hold close those who are dear, as they are your destiny,
Be the best you can be, and like yourself.
Let your destiny show who and what you are.

Jo Lodge

A Smile Made From Fairy Magic

A wee small tiny fairy, was indeed so very bored,
Thought one day of all the magic she had stored,
As you'll see she was indeed, so eloquently blessed,
So flew on a great and mighty magical, vast quest.

She thought to spread a smile, endless beautiful joy,
In every little child each world-wide girl and boy,
She imprinted a thought of laughter, every sweet child,
Giving a special magic seed, in each so meek and mild.

So it spread passing on in every new child's birth,
Surely spreading forever, using all her magic's worth,
This is why a new-born baby very often seems to smile
Because of this fairy spreading joy in such great style.

So you don't believe me, do you? Well you are wrong.
This is the very reason you're smiling, as you read along.
Don't say it's the cute thought that surely caused a grin,
'Twas this fairy's magic, planted in your heart within.

C R Slater

SIN HOLDS...

The tarnished gravestones
clinging to the shattered flowers that
grace the marble fountain. A chipped
and worn down golden engraving.
Holding in the stone the tears of towering
relatives that leave their prayers on top of empty boxes.
Glades of grass grow untouched, undisturbed . . .
Surviving where the feet of religious people
no longer step. The church bells rang . . . eroded,
left.
It seams to me, on no account of a bias view,
that the words of the bible evaporated . . . substituted
by science. Ran down the thin but toughened pages,
a collective political purity.
Mindset riots as we struggle to believe,
Enlightening our own diverse and fragile insecurity.
Religion held a promise of things to come . . .
Sin holds a promise of pleasure in the present.

Philip Naylor

THE LAST GOODBYE

It's very hard to say goodbye to someone that you love,
And send them to a better life, in Heaven high above.
The master's called your number, now you must swiftly go,
Is the life there better, who will ever know?
We never really took the time to say how much we cared,
Or talk about the boundless love the whole family shared.
The ones you've left behind must try to start anew,
And put aside the awful pain that came with losing you.
As the time flies swiftly by, the months turn into years,
And very, very, slowly, smiles replace the pain and tears.
One day we will meet up again when all our lives are through,
Until that day we must get on with doing what we do.

Vivienne Hudson-Lewis

Deliverance

she fell into
a drop of blood
and her world suddenly
brightened up
the colour was so vivid
playing with the light
in a rainbow of reds
now the shade of coral
now of vermilion
with, in-between
flashes of indigo
it felt so warm
that she believed
nothing could hurt her
anymore
and she was right
for the bullet
had reached her
smack between
her lovely blue eyes.

Albert Russo

A Picnic Unique

You don't remember! You don't remember anything!
But try -
Try to remember that picnic unique
In a glade
Surrounded by tall trees in gentle tremor
Sweet smell of green grass of meadow across
Little birds twittering and a squirrel playing hide-and-seek.

Try to remember -
That beaming sun, crimson rays breaching the boughs
Warming our Kashmir blanket of myriad colours
Champagne cork flying with a bang
Bigger than the 'Big Bang'
That sparkle of Asti Spumanti
Turkey sandwich and claret wine.

Try to remember -
The screech of a low flying, deafening Tornado
When you said, 'Go away, you interfering dragonfly.'
That butterfly with glee flapped its wings into our picnic -
Gentle breeze bristling your soft, velvet hair
And soothing my soul -
Those timid glances and eternal kiss -
Kiss! That kindled our love, passions flared.

Not so far away -
Remember the shadow of a figure
Of some guardian angel
Dressed in sable black, with bible in lap
Saying a prayer for you and I
For our love to last 'til eternity.

Try to remember -
That picnic - that was
'A picnic unique'.

A Jamil

TURBULENCE

The big one shakes silence
makes me glare
at overhead storage,
check seatbelt.

I breathe through my nose,
try not to imagine plane crashes
and last minutes
of a violent panic.

Barry Woods

Portrait Of The Artist

People will say we are in love
Because you laugh at my jokes
New black gloves just the job
Look over your shoulder, there's an angel behind you

People will find fault
Praise you till you ginger up
Or collect your dues for you
Pay you back on Mondays

Look good, feel good
Stand on ceremony
Make life worth living for all the world
Portrait of the artist as a young woman.

S M Thompson

Hurtful Memories

You said everything to hurt
You don't know the pain I
Feel it all too real
These words I need to say
Things are different in every way
As memories fade away
There are some things you cannot hide
Like the emptiness I feel inside
Sometimes you're not far from my mind
The past I thought I had left behind
Life has been so unkind
I have started anew
But without you
I still feel like a little girl lost
I left you all behind to my cost
Now after all the years
Come the tears
Gone is the humiliation
I hold my head up high
I did but try
The memories eventually will die
Things get better in time
I haven't committed a crime.

Samantha Groves

THE DREAM

I once had a dream,
To Heaven I would go
It was a very hard journey
Climbing the golden stair,
When I reached the top,
St Peter was there.

'Step forward, dear soul,
You come from where?'
'I come from Kesgrave,
In Suffolk,
Just down there.'

St Peter looked at me
With loving care,
But shook his head,
'You must return to Kesgrave,
For at the moment,
I have no room to spare.'

P Block

SKY

Spectacular sky, sceptre of the sun's shining splendour making mockery of mere man's meagre machinations to imitate its intensely intriguing imagery. Impressions crudely created on canvas, a cornucopia of colours consistently fail to fathom the fascination fanfare of fantasia's fabulous paradise. Parading, performing its perpetual pageant, a glittering gamut of gargantuan gaseous glory, gone so soon. Staying simply to share its sensuous sultry brilliance, biding only briefly before blithely bowing out. I try to trace this transient triumph of tempestuous nature, dying as darkness descends and drabness endures. Spectacular sky, sceptre of a most stupendous sun, stay!

Ali Paterson

HAD ENOUGH

I've had enough of night,
I've had enough of day.
I've had enough of living
my life this bloody way.
So many people angry with violent lives they lead,
kicking the hell out of someone then leaving them to bleed.
Scared to walk the streets when dark, or carry too much ash,
looking over our shoulders, in case we get a bash.
Young people's lives involve drugs or drink,
I personally think this country stinks.
By the time the police get there, the thug is long gone,
take it in your own hands then we're in the wrong.
I've had enough of justice;
I've had enough of law;
I've had enough of government
not doing bloody more.
We need to do something as it's getting out of hand,
I really think we should go make a stand.
When I was a teenager life was quite fun
we never had youngsters carrying guns.
Sex offenders being set free,
preying on children that they see.
Bring back the death penalty that's what we need,
then these monsters could no longer breed.

Mandy Jayne Moon

I'll Forever Love The Ones Close To My Heart But Forever Hate Everything About Me

You take the important things for granted
Family and love is all we need
That's unconditional even if the heart bleeds hate
Fate that will send us safely back when we are lost
No point fighting for some other lover's cheating cost

See I once misunderstood my family with all their love
cold as stone was all I remained looking for my own reply
But I can't and never will love myself for who I am
Though I hate what I've become I love my family for what they are
I tire of me, but never of them, I wish I was dead but I'd stay for them

I found a girl who loves me for me not somebody who's looking for
                                                                                 a play
Finally loved for being who I am, I love her and hope she can stay
I searched for love for what seems forever but I finally found my
                                                                                    true love
She is all that I hope for I just hope I can be her dream come true
Some of the clouds on my life are dividing and my hope is rebuilding

I may still hate all I feel for me but family's cause just keeps me going
It still hurts waking up to the same old pain I just can't be bothered still
I see my love laying next to me and I think of the family and continue
                                                                                        to live
Not every day can be a Saturday but to me every day's like a Monday
I can't quit I would I could kill me but I don't have that choice
                                                                                        any more

Besides I have a reason to live and that's something that has changed
For better or worse we will have to wait and see.

Jason Bone

LITTLE ME

Your mother has singed my best silk shirt, and burnt the apple crumble.
Last week she dropped that priceless vase, handed down through
generations, she's so clever with money, she has saved me a fortune.
How could we ever replace her?
I wonder why Daddy said that?

Your father is such an untidy man, he never folds up his pyjamas,
and on bath night sings at the top of his voice, whatever do the
neighbours think of us?
He is a tower of strength in a crisis. I could not live without him.
I wonder why Mummy said that?

Your grandmother is so house proud, not a cushion must be out of
place, but everything can be found in its right place, and dinner at 1
o'clock is always on time, she has been my best friend these last forty
years, what a treasure she has been to me.
I wonder why grandad said that?

Your grandad never wipes his boots on the mat, he brings half the
garden in with him, then there's that old pipe he smokes,
with ash all over the carpet, but on pension day, when he leaves the
house, with two busy roads to cross, I listen and wait, to hear the latch
of the gate and say, 'Thank God, he is back safe and sound.'
I wonder why Grandma said that?

To me it is simple, we all need each other, and love each other a lot.
There is one little thing they all seem to have forgotten,
because none of them could manage without *little me!*

Robert Warren

FLOWERS OF THE SPRING

Flowers of spring, rising higher and higher,
Growing in greatness like a wood-fed fire.

Petals spreading and showing their bliss,
Giving the sky a loving kiss.

Blossoms of scarlet, blue and red,
And purple and pink, laid out on their bed.

They're awakening and smiling because spring has arrived,
They're happy and bright because the winter has died.

Nikki Biram

AT THIS TIME

While we are sad
Our thoughts are of other times

We laughed and talked
The sun shone down

Remembering that smile
Making everything all right

Thoughts are our friends
We keep them in our hearts

Take them out when we will
Reassuring wonderful moments

Made for comforting
Have your happy moments

As time goes by.

Carole A Cleverdon

Money! (So What)

If I won the lottery, the football pools or a big premium bond,
Then the world would be my oyster, with possibilities that stretch
                                                               far beyond.
But I could not buy me happiness, extreme health nor a true love.
Happiness is, I've discovered, the greatest prize of all.
Health comes a close second, love, maybe a third.
I long to find true happiness, true love, a peace and calm life,
A world of tranquillity, no fighting or greed.
Always thought that money was all I'd ever need.
This year I'm going on a quest to find hopefully the elusive thing
                                                   called happiness.
Try my utmost, do whatever I can, learn about life, truth, my
                                                   fellow man.
Will I find what I yearn for?
Who knows, not I.
Hope to find an inner peace, love, but mostly my happiness.
Costs nothing, but I think it is a great treasure,
One to hang onto, pledge to keep.

Susan Barker

THE BEGGAR

The beggar's arms outstretched, pleading to each and every passer-by
believe you me his take-home earnings are way above those
                                                    of you and I!
His words encourage more generosity upon the next coming of
                                                      the Messiah
hoping that by touching your conscience the donation will be
                                                      much higher.
Year in, year out he squats in the same rags, with filth cemented on
                                                    once-white skin
but as the hush of evening falls he hops into his limousine with a
                                                    knowing grin.
On the outskirts of the city is a marbled palace with all the luxuries
                                                        one desires
the beggar slips into silken robes, drinks his cognac and waits for the
                                                      day he retires.

Lorraine Cohen

HAVE A NICE DAY

Open your eyes and see butterflies,
The shapes of leaves, the wind that sighs,
Then prick your ears to songs of birds,
And cast off blinkers, speak kind words.

You look at faces that pass and smile,
Say hello, having walked a mile,
Then laugh and breathe in deep the air,
The morning's bright so don't despair.

Relax your muscles stressed and tight,
And feel the warmth of morning light,
You're living, laughing, so in love,
So sing a song and look above.

When day is done, exhausted, flat,
Go shower quickly, have a chat,
And talk of string and sealing wax,
Then home to bed and sleep, relax.

So sweet your dreams, you slumber doze,
On pillows soft, you rest, repose,
Midnight approaches, deep your sleep,
Until the morning's chorus leaps.

David M Walford

Outside Crown Court No 5, Manchester

Graphite she glides black on white, white on black,
Proud-browed and cold as the marble she strides.
Gown torn floats, just, tattered wings in the streams
Of frosty airs exhaled without effort.
Eschewing our gaze, she passes us by,
Now world, no smile, nor frown to acknowledges
Our interest - her eye is fixed far beyond.
From sight she leaves us to bathe in her scent,
Rich, exclusive and unobtainable.

Mark A Holbrook

JUST GRACE

Auburn touching fair
Petite, trim and smart
But that's not all
It's just that look
That impish little smile
The glee that ripples into laughter
And touches everything . . .
Down to a depth
so serious
It's known to God alone . . .
Of spirit and of mind
Of present, future, past
Of hopes and dreams
And courage strong
To stay the fight
And win.

Joan Bennett

The Evolving Nap

Today,
the sky is grey;
mixtures of the absence
of colour
and my eyes look
through the lace
of barren maple tree,
for anything that resembles life.
Winter's voice speaks loudly
and yet, there is no sign
of snow.
The fire is roaring
and I feel
a nap evolving.
Rubbing my eyes,
tossing my hair
upon my pillow,
I look
outside my window
and drift away
into the land
where dreams are made.

Carla Iacovetti

AUTUMN NIGHT

The air is still
She greets me with her open arms
Wraps me up in silence
Seduces me with her chilling charm

Beneath these open skies
On marble-shaped clouds the moon's rays hit
The steely moon, shining its hypnotising light
On which the angels sit.

I walk on and through
The leaves' rustling I hear
The wind calls out and weaves silently
Through the trees that are near.

Autumn is here
Summer has gone
As one season leaves the world's stage
The curtain draws as another comes on.

Rob Hallsworth

As We Leave Years Of Footprints Behind Us On The Sand

Seven years is too long
Dexy's even sung about it in a song
Soon we have to meet
On the sand as we promised
Walking with no shoes on our feet
Two glasses and a bottle of Blossom red
Sharing the company with whoever is watching us from the sea bed.

Moon guiding us along the way
Laughing
And joking,
And talking,
We have so much to say.
Lady,
I am at your command
Hold me tighter
As we stroll, hand in hand
The night-time breeze
Is oh, so cool
Holding my shirt in my hand
As we leave years of footprints
Behind us on the sand.

The night is young
And once so were we
As we stand looking into the ocean
Underneath a palm tree
We talk and we laugh
Reminisce about the past
But I hope now that you know
We did it.
What we said we would do
Seven years ago.

Sorry but it's time to say goodbye
As we steal one more look from each other's eyes
I walk with you back to your rented car
You thinking up an alibi
As I walk back along the edge of the sea in the dark
But remember forever we will be
Friends and reminisce of our night by the sea
Love does have many different faces
I still have to find one that belongs to me.

Stephen A Owen

THIS GENERATION HAS NO NATION

Why can't she come in?
Prefer, they would
For dark crimson blood
To mark her previous constraints

He walks on streets of gold
As the masses stop to stare and comment
On how his shirt apparently reeks of expense
Taking the 'taxes from underneath our noses'.

I cannot see
These flashing neon lights
That apparently indicate foreboding sensations
If only we were all as blind as me

To reveal the decadence
Of our supposed free world
Would be just as
Hypercritical as the mongrel masses

Capitalists throttle frontiers
Decay fosters in motorised vehicles
Pride instilled in the new system
Pride in death and sin

I hope the manifestioni
Heighten the ruckus of disdain
Claim back the rules of humanity
Naiveté of love, hope and freedom to stay.

Onyeka Igwe

As One

I feel the earth
beneath my feet.
Your spirit, my soul entwine
I learn to feel
the things you feel
and cherish all that's mine.
The air I breathe
love, faith and hope
are all I need to go on.
A fire in my heart
and deep down inside
will forever keep me strong.

Donna Davies

THE PHOENIX

'I am she,'
she spoke out loud,
'arisen from the flames,
you wronged me once
and broke my world
leaving me alone
to drown in all my pain.'
Her glory flickered wildly
with dignity that reigned,
determination healed her wounds,
it's love that she would save.
'I stand here out of ashes
which you would have made my grave,
to me you are forgiven
and whom that I will pray.'
Her spirit showered colours
as she started down a road,
free among her wishes
and dreams that she is owed.
'You will never take me,'
defiantly she flew,
'despite that you may crush my body
I will rise anew.
You can never stop me dreaming
or cease beliefs I hold
for I'll remain unbreakable
in my immortal soul.'

Rosalind Cook

5 Minutes

Cancer   hangs   at the bar
A fag fug of fog
Thick aroma of carcinoma
Infuse the little stick with the long fuse
Burning at both ends
Internal combustion with silent explosion
Selfish, cylindrical, suicide bomber
Cough, hack, asthma attack
Spray killing kids
A patch can't repair
One lung out
One silk cut from thigh to collar bone
'They're not doing that again!'
Once was one of
Twenty players lined up
Waiting for the buzz, the high, the rushing roulette
Firing squad ready
For the quick draw
Five minutes
Gone
Another one stubbed out.

S McKinlay

AMH

I love working, when Lyn phones,
which helps to pay off all my loans!
In a very friendly environment,
part-time inputter for the local government!

'AMH, can I help you?'
staff say, answering people on 'phone queues'.
'Please could I go on your mailing list?'
(Public). 'And send me information, which is the latest!'

'The Arts' are in the same room,
most are happy and never gloom!
Some like the football team *'Saints'*
Others, just have to deal with the complaints!

All of the adults love sweets,
which is normally a special treat!
So: Aida, Lyn, John, Leo, James, Adelaide and Arti,
and all, try not to eat too many Smarties!

Barry Ryan

GOLD

She is haunted by a whispering breeze.
Back bent with the weight of age,
Beneath a halo of summer brightness,
Shining all about her as she picks flowers;
Their golden petals touched by falling tears,
As they tremble in her withering hands,
Remind her of once golden locks,
Now thinned and grey;
Shadows of time hanging about her face.

The halo brightens further.
She feels a lightness of being
As the flowers tumble from her hands in silence,
To fall at her feet as she topples,
Body collapsing to lie motionless in the sun,
The golden aspect finding liberty;
She is innocent once more.

Edwin Page

DAUGHTER, WITNESS, GANG WAR

Stay here.
Be good.
Your coarse voice scrapes my ears like
the unmerciful pavement that grinds your skin.

Neon blue, pink, green, yellow
seduces you from silhouette of night
as I - my eyes - trace your footsteps
left and right
from the safety of our backstreet covert.

Tears - like a kaleidoscope -
distorts and mollifies
your violence into something as sweetly bitter
as that melted bar of chocolate
you placed into my hands.

Ain't they your friends?
But now all I see from my side of this liquid dream
are flashes from your heavy sabre
and vivid red staining your hands.
Then
My world swirls like cigarette smoke
as a battle cry of death breathes on my leaping heart and
a blade oh-so-easily pierces through yours.

Your eyes
glassy yet more opaque than marbles in my pocket
see nothing, see me not.
A cold body, a wan, sad face.
A daddy no more.

Vickie Lui

SEASCAPE

Somewhere between the lighthouse and the beach
I sensed a shifting of the coastal light.
The sky began to lose its brazen blue;
An oyster-catcher's bill seemed not quite right.
The sea-pinks aged in seconds, turning drab.
Two ravens' feathers paled to shades of slate.
Bold yellow ragwort leeched away its warmth
And sand grew dull like burnt ash in the grate.

We walked along an undulating path,
As stifled as the sullen summer air.
Green was the colour of your jaded eyes,
Reflected in my own like fading care.
For all that's said about its being black,
I learned that grey's the colour of despair.

Tom Valentine

Last Whispers

The time is drawing near, my love
I know you want to stay
I'd sell my soul for any bid
To buy you one more day

I know you're on a journey soon
A journey I can't share
I want to walk beside you love
Instead I stand and stare

My instinct is to shout, my love
My instinct is to scream
To cry on high, 'It's just not fair!
Why can't this be a dream?'

Instead I have to whisper, love
Instead I have to quell
The angry voice that twists my heart
That cries out . . . *bloody hell!*

I'll go to bed alone tonight
You'll not be by my side
No whispered voice will soothe me now
When I cry out in fright

But here we lie now, hand-in-hand
Our talking nearly done
It's been a battle long, my love
And this one we've not won

I'll pray for you each night, my love
I have no other choice
I'll beg the angels grant me dream
I once more hear your voice

So, soft my love, let go the fight
Reach gentle for the door
I'll whisper quiet in your ear
Until you hear no more.

Peter Elliott

Fond Memories

I recollect the heartaches in this life of mine
Including my sorrows memorised through time
And so many lovely people by fortune that I've met
Who have helped me to progress? Plus keep me out of debt
Happy times in plenty, and to weddings I would rush
Birthdays, anniversaries, holidays, travelling in the crush
Friends and relations who are known in this life
Lots of little milestones, some of them brought strife
And over all the years some friends kept in touch
Others simply vanished, disappearing in the dust
One wonders what happened, 'Where are they living now?'
Do they remember me still, with feelings of great joy?
Sometimes class reunions, delved back again to youth
We all must go forward, and that is the constant truth
The highs and the lows we meet with, is a story about living
Never-ending improvements in work to which driven
Speeds taken over faster, and fast we spin the wheel
The great wheel of fortune might so increase our dreams
While lotteries and horse races, quick ways of getting rich
Sporting all our favourites and thereby comes the hitch
Contentment with life and what we have achieved
Can be shared with others, and those in greater need
We should live in this life, full of its speedy manoeuvres
To slow down just a little, and give some help to others.

Joan Prentice

Noughts And Crosses

How I wish, when as a boy at school
    I had not been such a feckless fool,
And had somehow managed to find
    A way to instil arithmetic in my mind,
But a mystery it remains, and try as I will,
    Enlightenment escapes me still,
Trying to solve even the simplest calculation
    Fills me with dread and trepidation.
For although Euclid no doubt explained why,
    I still can't grasp what equals pi . . .
As for the concept of a fourth dimension,
    That's something way beyond my comprehension.
Why did those ancient Greek fanatics
    Have to plague the world with mathematics,
Compelling simple folk like me to grapple
    With a mind boggling, never-ending battle.
Human wits are ill equipped to agree
    With Einstein and his theory of relativity.
What tortuous mind first decreed
    That geometry and trigonometry was what we need?
As for algebra, 'tis a torture designed to confuse
    And cause the brain to blow a fuse.
As I reflect, in retrospect I can see
    Why I and figures can never agree,
Though I tackle sums with fierce concentration,
    The result is nought but sheer frustration,
So I've given up trying now, and turn away
    From this Devil's work and have to say
That problems of multiplication and division
    Are best left to others for their decision.

F R Smith

MY DREAMS

Memories of my many dreams
Transport me into satisfaction, actually hurled
I think back to my former schemes
And am transposed into a lovely world.
Glowing the sky, red the sunset at night
Also glowing the hot midday sun
The stars that shone so bright,
And the moonlight faintly just begun.
Mountains towering over my head,
Such white snow making many a fatality.
I glory in these memories not dead
Even if some are dreams of reality.
Now I must remember all of them, I'll explain
For never can I experience them truly, again.

Marj Busby

I Shall Write!

I move
My wrist
And I shall write
Whatever the moment
Day or night
But not for me
A question
To ask
I am the servant
So it's best
I serve
And do
My task.

High Priest

ONE-NIGHT STAND

Over coffee
And toast,
We never spoke.
The alcohol out
Of our system:
The night before
Long gone; she
Had that look
On her face, it
Had been wrong.
She left on high heels
Taking her broken ideals.
Funny, I couldn't
Remember her name!
Was it Janet or Jane?

Alan Holdsworth

I Am This Dream

I'm closing my eyes now,
Can you see me?
I'm closing my mind now,
Can you hear me?
I'm dreaming now,
Far away,
A hand has lifted this body of mine,
Carries me on a cloud,
Far from here,
Far from fear and anger in the streets.
I'm above it all,
Looking down,
I am this dream,
Are you with me?
Together we glide
Through a velvet sky,
To a place where my dreams are true.
I'm awake now,
Eyes open,
I'm here with you.

Richard Ward

THE RAILWAY STATION

Mr Tannoy Man with his nasal tones announcing the comings
and goings.
Have I got a penny for my platform ticket?
The guard he does just that, no one allowed through without a ticket
to receive or one to leave.
Always a draught as I look down the line, at lengths and lengths
of track.
Forged solid steel and sleepers that never seem to sleep.
Peppered by lumps of ebony coals, escapees from the0 shovel.
The stench of grease and cooled hot steam hangs in the air.
Trunks and parcels stacked on trolleys, I wonder where they are off to?
I dig deep into my pocket whilst I wait; the fry's chocolate machine
looks tempting.
Whistles blowing, flags are waved, many a door is slammed.
Squeals on the tracks as engines fight to stop.
Billows of steam fluff into the skylights nudging the roosting birds.
Time stands still I'm sure, you know, the station clock never seems
to move.
An announcement from the crackling box diverts all eyes down
the track.
I can see an engine slowing down, screaming against the steel.
Clouds of smoke pour from the funnel as the engine is all chuffed out.
I'm not waiting for the first or second-class today but the guard's van
at the back.
For amongst the straw, goats and bicycles is a parcel from Uncle Jack.

Mary Morley

Not Quite Right
(Dedicated to Abbi and Jennie, friends out of a time that has been so difficult to recapture)

Desperate threads we long to grasp,
Yet always out of reach.
That once we held so dear, so close,
But now the ends no longer meet.

Life long dead we revive in vain,
A tainted parody.
Twisted corpse of past delight,
No place in our reality.

Warped reflections, at which we stare,
Something's just not right.
Just copies of our former glory,
Defects too wrong to try to right.

Tiffany Little

GRANNY SPUDS

Oh Granny dear, please don't cry,
You're not insane to me,
But all these spuds that you buy,
No reason's plain to see.

This house of mine drove me mad,
It's caked and stained in blood.
For years ago in its place,
An orphanage once stood.
The little ones that they took there,
With no love or next of kin,
Would starve or maybe freeze to death,
Their weeps heard from within.
As I'm alone and all is sound
In my calm serenity,
Their meagre lives in ghostly form
Survive by haunting me.
I tried for years to comfort them,
But never quite enough,
All my feeble efforts made,
My warmth, my tears and love.

Still, all these spuds that you buy,
No reason's plain to me.

You stupid fool, it's obvious,
They all love chips you see.

M Illsley (Cambo)

They Cannot Speak

Man's machine rolls on relentless
The forest dies and the ocean too
The wilderness is not in plan
Our captive minds prefer the zoo

Human kind that are so shallow
Seek only exploitation and abuse
Gentleness, love and beauty give way
To human comfort and animal use

Would the Father send his Son
Among animals that he did not love?
For they have made the ultimate sacrifice
Given their flesh to nurture us.

In the winter cold and starving
Children crying, blessed mother weak
The animals were slaughtered
Gentle trusting friends that could not speak.

Why then now, with crops aplenty
Corn, fruit and vegetables of every kind
Do we still persist to eat the flesh
Of blessed creatures, pure of mind.

Roy Baker

SHADOWS AND REFLECTIONS

Just being alive we make our sacrifice and find ourselves
amidst the strife of survival, in search of the universal.
Only casualties emerge in this living rehearsal.
Playing our part in the carnival with the heart of a wounded animal.
Touched, by all things physical.

Our dreams are the enchantment of starlight, passions in flight
Light spilling over the horizon, catching a cool air of wisdom.
We wait for our vision to be realised to see with our own eyes,
hopes unfolding
A transition of becoming for belonging, instinct and feeling
for what we can hold and experience.

These punctuation marks of living . . . the foundations of our
                                                          expression,
that mould our impressions of resistance and persuasion
Night-time brings freedom from the logic of reason,
liberty for dreaming.
Imagination riding wild on the wings of fortune.

Stirring winds whisper of change in the heavens,
opening doors to new dimensions.
Knowledge growing form its own meaning blossoms.
Clouds form like fashion, drifting in the rise and fall of natural patterns
Sensational rhythms build in waves to new heights of perception,
that breaking on the shores of our ambitions.
Twisting emotions in vibrant animation that spiral
in a timeless evolution of something and nothing.

Justin Lowe

FROM MAD WE CAME AND TO MAD WE RETURN

But before that we all should have a good life.
We have to fight a big battle to survive
And to have a decent life.
It is not so easy for many people
To live nicely and splash money here and there.
Most of the people struggle to have bread and butter,
And some do burn their money
Because they have too much of it.
It seems unfair to the rest of the poor people
In this difficult world.
Some could say why does God allow
The rich to do extravagant things,
While the poor cannot buy that
Which is most necessary for their children?
Because we have so many greedy people.
God did give the same chance to all of us.
The poor will all be compensated
In the new kingdom of God's new world.
It will happen sooner than you think.
If it is any consolation, we are all the same in the end.
Dust to dust, and mud to mud?
Dead is equal, rich and poor.
I beg to God to bless us all.

Antonio Martorelli

TIME TO OURSELVES

In the saddest twilight
known to man or woman,
find no sweeter omen
than the sigh of a wistful virgin
left to watch birds fly
(too high to identify)
sailing the fairest horizon,
teasing the inner eye;
O, beauty, mystery,
such privileges of passion!
Glimpses of Heaven;
no word of invitation, nor
greater loneliness known
than each of us, a secret
celebration, our
kingdom come.

R N Taber

FEELINGS

I remember how it used to be
So many years ago
The feelings that swelled up in me
My heart was all aglow

The excitement when I saw you
My pulse began to race
I hurried home to greet you
With your handsome, smiling face

Time has changed those feelings
We're companions, friends you see
But it doesn't stop me remembering
How it felt once for you and me.

Jo Seward

UNTITLED

Don't try to get inside my mind
You may not like what you will find

Grey clouds shadow what used to be bright
That keeps you awake all through the night

You finally give in, exhaustion takes over
Twitching, turning, dreaming a lot
Of climbing a hill but never reaching the top

Alarm bells ring, it's time you awake
Your head is so heavy, your body just aches

Your first thoughts on waking
'Thank God I'm alive'
I put my hands together and pray
'Dear God, please help me get through today'

The hum of machines, voices, music,
The jingle of keys
You break down in despair,
Hands cover your ears

You've entered the tunnel
There's no going back
Your wheels are not turning
They've stopped on the track

It's a long and lonely time ahead
Of panic and of fears
How will you see the light
With your eyes filled with tears?

Fatigue takes over, it feels like you're drowning
Your heart skips a beat
Then it starts pounding

You fear you are ill
Obsessed you will die
You're assured you won't
You ask yourself why

Why do I hurt from my head to my toe?
Why do I feel so much sorrow and woe?
It's not just a feeling of being under the weather
Please don't say, 'Pull yourself together.'

One day my mind will heal
And take away the pain
I'll live my life just as I should . . .
I'll smile once again.

Jayne Evans

TEDDY

The house is quiet
Our dog has just died
How can we replace him?
He always did us proud
The sad thing is
We killed him
By feeding him too well
We really did kill him
And now we deserve this hell
We hope he's in dog heaven
We will meet him one day
When we have to give an account
Of all our ways.

Mary Tickle

Untitled

Quiet dreams
In seclusion
Quiet streams
Of delusion
Voices and pictures
Idle in my mind
Choices and victors
Cradled upon time.

Philip Allen

HEATHER

H   stands for all the help you gave so true.
E   stands for those twinkling eyes of brown.
A   stands for being so loving and adorable.
T   stands for the tears you shed for me.
H   stands for the hugs and kisses you gave.
E   stands for the elation my heart feels when you are near.
R   stands for right and right you will always be.

Join these precious letters together
and you'll have a name that means so much to me.

My loving daughter, God bless.

Nancy Elliott

WHAT WILL I BE?

The mines and factories have closed
And new technologies are coming
Along to bring a new life of hope
For our communities.

We can use our skills
And education to build
A better life.
Benefits will support families.
There is anger, frustration
And people are distressed
About the future.
What will I be?
What will I think or feel?
It depends on God
And faith, hope and love.

Kenneth Mood

DREAMS

Deep in your sleep,
They feel so real,
They cause you to cry,
They cause you to scream,
Why do dreams feel so real?
Is it another world that we feel?
You awake halfway through,
Then try to go back,
They will not let you,
The dream has lost its appeal.
Dreams can be good and bad,
Adventurous, scary and cold,
Frightening, loving and bold,
If only these dreams could come true,
I will always be dreaming
Of a wonderful person like you.

Maggie Hickinbotham

GARDEN

The earth of my garden is hard and frosty cold
My toes within my boots are tightly nipped and closed,
Like Brussels buds close clinging to a frozen host they lie, upon
A swollen stem bowed down with darkened grief
And shiver in a misery. Ready to be picked.

My toes are cold. Stiff, as a forgotten row of peas.
Pods sown late in the haste of summer, surplus and forgotten.
Now iced today in brittle hardness
Desperately clinging to a blackened stem. Ready to be snapped.

No squelchy warmth of dampened soil to warm the cold within.
My spade, as sharp as a fencer's blade
Can't pierce the ground to let the flow of hot black blood
Come coursing through her veins. Ready to be sown.

The earth of my garden is cold and hard
The ice has settled well.
The sky may lighten and the rooks may rook,
The sap my rise and the rose may bloom
But the dark of my winter will never end. Ready now to die.

Clare Saffell

Do You Want To Go To Ireland?

Come hold my hand dear
And I'll take you to Ireland's land
Where the laughing Irish eyes
Will make your smile expand
We'll walk the Giant's Causeway
And swim in Galway Bay
Visit Dublin fair city
And have a drink in Killyleagh
We'll kiss the famous Blarney Stone
And climb St Patrick's mound
Gather shamrock, clover and heather
That you'll see as we walk around
We'll listen to the fiddle
And tap our toes to reels
Dance with all the leprechauns
That's in dear Ireland's fields
The poteen and the whiskey
Will make us dance with joy
We'll have a good old singsong
And have a go at Danny Boy!
We'll go to Doherty's hooley
Sit around the big open fire
Smell the turf and watch the logs
As the flames dance higher and higher
We'll hear some yarns of days gone by
From Ireland's oldest folk
Have a belly laugh or two
When we hear Dan Morgan's jokes
And when the night is over
And we go down to sleep
You'll hear the banshee in the night
So don't you stir or peep!

Just close your eyes till morning
You'll know you are awake
You'll have a great big hangover
And your poor old head will ache!

Geraldine McMullan Doherty

REALLY

I know you won't believe it but I have to say,
I saw an elephant with glasses on earlier today.
When walking later on, do you know what I saw?
An ostrich with galoshes and a rain hat that's for sure.
Normally I don't notice just what passes me by,
Like this large orang-utan leaping through the sky.
I'll sit down here and rest a while, think I'll have my lunch,
Good heavens, where did they come from, bananas in a bunch.
What on earth is this I see getting closer towards me?
I think I should get up and move before it gets to close.
Too late, the big bear is in my face and touching my nose.
Oh my body will not move, I cannot scream and shout,
If I'm in a nightmare, will someone get me out?
His tongue is warm and wet, it's scratching on my cheek,
I can't get up to run, my body is too weak.
Is no one going to rescue me, am I to meet my end?
His rasping tongue does not tickle and is not my friend.
Someone is running, hey, I'm over here.
'Don't worry lady, he is a grand old bear.
He must have seen the sandwiches and that juicy pear . . .'
Then all at once I was at home, woken by the phone,
I looked through my window and guess what I could see?
A great big giraffe waving its tail at me . . .

Ellen Chambers

In The Desert

In this desert, thirsty for the rain of
love and understanding, standing staring
at miles of uncaring space, despairing
for the decency of the human race,
I pray for an end to the loneliness.
Left in the blazing heat of hatred's sun,
with all hope stolen by my past mistakes,
Satan holds me at the point of a gun
waiting to see my resilience break.
Can I find the cool shade of affection,
drink from the tap of life's resurrection?
Or am I destined to die here alone
in misery, with no one there to cry?

Clive E Oseman

MOUNTAINOUS TRIUMPH

I want to delve into reading but my eyes get in the way
I want to listen to music, but at present, my head gets in the way
I want to have peace and seclusion, but amongst my mates in town
But, I'm being crushed by society and the way it effects my own
Society has a story, it finds its own through the scriptures of life
It sings and it dances, and it prances wrongs and the rights
I'm going to find that mountain, even if it's only in my head
Rest, and do my own thing, just as my granddaughter once said
My pen will start to scribe the lessons, for me and for my mates
None of them will realise, for sometimes they don't adhere
Sometimes they do not see, sometimes they don't hear
Sometimes although they can see and hear, they are deafer and
                                                              blinder than me

  Society is the instigator that causes terrorist war
  Then we as people either cry wolf or not worry at all
  But whatever takes place in this sorry world of ours
  There will always be sanctuary, for it is there to be had by all
  Let us all pray that life helps us with hope
  That each and every one of us, can become a stronger person
  That Earth and all its finery, will have a better home
  The universe and its love for all its people unknown
  I want to delve into reading, but my mind tells it all
  I want to listen to music, I will, for it has beauty to tell
  I want peace, I can smile for it is there
  And so society that does crush, it can take a swim -
  One day then, the truth will be known.

Josie Lawson

WEDDING DRESS

Once upon a midnight dream
Shadows, playing tricks on the wall
Memories looming, in desperate plight
Trying to communicate with the past
For answers that might not be there
And forgotten love that didn't last
From a lover that didn't care
Reaching out, she cried in vain
Her torment still lingers on
Still waiting for her love to come again
Waiting for her lover, never to come
Alone she sits in her wedding dress
Old age now takes her life
Walking alone in her wilderness
Never to have been a wife
She calls out from beyond her grave
To a lonely woman in the night
Trying to save another woman's life
Perhaps this time she can get it right.

Tina Nightingale

Bath Night

Burning, glowing full of warmth
Red-hot coals on fire bright
Children standing in its glow
Casting shadows on the wall
Giving light to dreary room.
Old tin bath in corner stands
Steams with hot and soapy water
Saturday night is bath night
Cleansing of the body
Uplifting of the soul.

Candlelight to see the way
Candescent glow upon the stairs
Make animal shapes upon the walls
Childish laughter of joy and mirth
Sweet-smelling children
To dreamland go
As they follow the mesmeric light.

D E Henry

Mind, Body And Soul

With thoughts produced in stereo
Our twin bulbs always dim or glow
In unison, as if they shine
Encompassed by a single mind.

A physical addiction which
Has heated up to fever pitch.
From budding passions thence to find
Immutable the drives that bind.

A common future will be shared,
The starry heavens jointly fared
For I am yours as you are mine;
Eternal spirits intertwined.

Chris Scriven

TAKANANO

A lake found her frozen
Broken and used by life
She purposely returned to die
To a place once with her lover
She felt free and alive
The lover returned to America
She, was again, left alone
And if not for the slow news day
None would have heard
Of the Japanese girl Takanano
Who they sensationally said,
'Was looking for money!'
Which was never found in the plot
Of a 'Cohen Bros' movie
In a film and city called 'Fargo'
None of it was true
So she walked out into the cold
Like an old American Indian chief
To remember her life and to die in the snow.

Phil Roberts

THE THIN RED LINE

I was an Argyll and Sutherland Highlander
Of the famous 'Thin Red Line'
And was proud to wear the tartan
During the war of thirty-nine.

The red and white dice on their Glengarry
Showed the plan they had in mind,
With the red dice depicting the forward troops,
Whilst the white dice was in behind.

The Russian guns kept pounding them,
But the Highlanders didn't flee,
They kept filling up their broken ranks
Until they won victory.

The battalion won the VC here
For heroics of the few,
The Russians never understood
How they couldn't be subdued.

But Highland troops are brave and bold
And never lack the nerve,
This is why they receive the accolades
Which brave accomplishments deserve.

Lachlan Taylor

WAITING

Waiting . . . waiting . . . no point worrying . . .
They said they'd phone when they got home.
We'd agreed, no sense in hurrying;
Long journey when you live in Rome . . .

Waiting . . . listening . . . now past midnight . . .
On going out, 'Don't wait up,' she'd said.
She's with good friends, she'll be all right . . .
Can't sleep though, 'til she's home in bed.

Waiting . . . while anticipating
Whatever news the surgeon brings;
Must be good . . . not contemplating
Complications, or any such things.

Waiting . . . pretending not to care . . .
Six weeks now since the last exam . . .
Yet wondering how at worst he'll fare?
He needs that place at Birmingham.

Waiting . . . hours . . . pacing up and down . . .
Nurse has said, 'Not long now. All's well.'
Must stop behaving like a clown,
And listen hard for babe's first yell.

Waiting . . . dreading the dentist's chair . . .
Old magazines are no distraction.
Much longer now and I'll despair . . .
Hope just a filling, not extraction.

Waiting now is over . . . next day
Anxieties are of the past.
The call from Rome came through OK.
The daughter came home safe - at last!

The surgeon had good news to tell.
Exam results were almost thrilling!
Both mother and son are doing well,
And treatment was just tiny filling!

Time waits for no man, so it's said,
So man must wait for time - 'til dead.

Geoffrey Matthews

OH, WHATEVER WILL BE

I saw a heron fly up from the field
and by a wooden shack
rats scurrying
under the boards
we went into an empty building
and I chanted Om
and a few other expletives.
That journey down a road
outside of Graylingwell Hospital
with a trained naturalist
opened my eyes up
to the things
that man hasn't altered
it is a shame that nature
has no say
I wonder if the world
is crazy
or whether I have lost my mind
down a road
that no one visits anymore.
So on my way back from you
who peruse these lines
realise you have no name
I can define
your existence fluctuates
in the same way a butterfly
dances gold circles
around the moon.

Dave St Clair

BOB MONKHOUSE

His career began in 1953 with the Goon Show,
Which still leaves in our hearts a happy, warm glow.
Later on, Bob hosted quiz shows,
He gave to many of us joy,
And now he dwells with the master
In the skies of paradise.

David A Bray

VESUVIO

There's a soldier buried on Vesuvio
A friend, a prisoner of war
Who was captured in 1944

He missed his family desperately
The sun, the friendliness
He called Mum, his second mamma
She knew no enemies
She was a Red Cross nurse

He came and had tea and chatted
In broken English and we laughed
Played his records of Gigli
Which he bought me
He had earned from his craft

One day he was repatriated on May 16, 1946
He gave me a jewel box carved by hand
At Kew Gardens, before he returned to his sunny land

He said, 'One day you come to Italy.'
We said, 'Yes, one day, perhaps.'
But conditions were hard after a war
And we had to face the facts

Christmas cards were exchanged
For many a long year
Our daily lives improved
Governments came and went
Buildings grew and grew
Old ones removed

Then years later in 1963
My cousins asked me, Joan, come to Italy
We saw our friend and his mamma and his papa

His wife and Palmina his daughter
And returned with wonderful memories
Of Pompeii, Vesuvio, Amalfi, Vietri, Ravello,
Capri and Positano

It was like being in a lavender mist
These sights were new to me
Brilliant light and warmth enveloped my soul
And I felt whole
Pompeii made me feel life eternal
I felt I would live forever
Later to find how fate decides
And what a long time is never

So we came again to Sorrento
After many a long year
Minus our loved ones
Only to find that our dear friend had died suddenly
Just before we arrived here

So we look at Vesuvio and we shed a tear
And remember our friend buried there
In his beloved Italy
He gave us laughter, and gave us tears
And in England he will be remembered
For many a long year.

J Cashford

A Dying Wish

They all said this would come quick
an unexplainable pain that could make one sick
Past visions start to flow back to me
But no one stands welcome how can this be
Past told stories of a welcoming hand
But all I see is death where I should stand
Give us this day the light for the dead
How can this help if it is all in one's head
I think of you on this darkening day
As my life force slowly slips away
War was supposed to be filled with honour and pride
And I was told that God would always be by my side
But as I look at the bullet-filled skies
I find no meaning; let it be known I've tried
On this darkening day I can say no more
As more and more bodies hit the floor
If they have suffered the same fate as I
We'll never know as I take one last blink of my eye
I take one last thought of how this land used to be
Before the bullets there was a time of prosperity
But times have changed, and bullets fly
As more and more people unnecessarily die
Why do we fight for someone who sits miles away
When their proclaimed democracy failed to keep war at bay
They will send a grieving letter of my passing soul
But what comfort can be found with this ultimate toll
And as the light turns to dark
I think of the journey that you shall embark
I wish upon wish for one last moment with you
Maybe if I believe I can make it come true.

Peter W J Baxter

THE WIDOW

Sitting beneath her fireside kettle on the boil,
Sadly her hubby, Big Jamie,
Will not be coming home.
No more broad smiles, flowers from
God knows where.
The kisses and cuddles, excuses for being late. Agh!
Sure his heart was as big, the silly old fool,
Not a word of anger passed his lips.
Always kind and gentle,
This was his way.
How did I ever stand the smell
Of those size 10 feet?
At the local jig, Jamie had no peers.
A tango or a rumba he did excel.
Alas no more Jamie for the last dance for me.
I'm sure that in Heaven he leads all a merry dance.
God I wish he was beside me, warts and all.
We buried him in his Sunday best,
A rose on his chest,
As handsome as the day we wed.
That was my big Jamie.
Goodnight my darling,
I'll see you in my dreams
And when God bids my time,
We will be together again.

Norman Andrew Downie

A Ward Of The Moon

Heartaches are built
Of fond memories
Tears are the remnants of love
Lonely arms are the cradle now empty
That once rocked an angel above
Her cute little dimples
I pine for
The odd roving pimple or two
Of finest rolled gold
Were her ringlets
Framing a heavenly view
For three precious years
I would hold her
Her chuckles would echo the room
But our good Lord
Had special plans for her
And made her a ward of the moon.

B Wardle

WET, WET, WET!

There are days when it's best
Not to dress.
There are days when it's best
In bed.

When the rain plays music
In the drainpipe outside
And the sun behind clouds
Decides it will hide
When the eyes are bleary
And the head is weary

Well - there are days when rest
Is the *best!*

Lyn Sandford

ALL SOULS' DAY

Lovely ladies, like
of old,
clutching at umbrellas like
troopers at their parachutes, with looks like
weeping windscreen wipers.

Timothy McNeal

I Miss You

I remember our first wartime meeting in the library,
and how nonchalantly you pretended not to notice me,
and how your glances and your sparkling eyes so distracted me.
I still cannot believe that you are gone.
I can still recall our springtime visit to Trafalgar Square
and our first kiss, which was curtailed by air-raid sirens through the air.

Today I wake to find an empty bed and no one laying there.
Through the window shines an opaque winter sun.
If I could only talk to you and hear your voice again,
We would link our arms to walk the streets of Streatham Hill again
(would you mind the rain?)
But I know that is not possible, to dream is all in vain,
I have to go to work now, darling, so it's goodbye once again.

I know that when the spring comes, in the greenery
(of an old familiar place where stands that same oak tree)
The flowers will bloom, the birds return from their warm migratory,
in my heart it will be winter still, cold and dark eternally.
I miss you desperately.

Keith W Hewett

ALICE

I traced her lips
The ruby lips
That told
A thousand lies

Moist and full
Knowing well
She had robbed
A million souls

Smoke and
Coffee stains
yellowing satin
Trapped musty
Smell caught
In a tatty
Cardboard box

White and well cut
It glinted in her eye
Then swung loosely
Around her
Wrinkled finger

Alice bruises easily
But shows no guilt.

Moira Jean Clelland

Lovers' Silhouette

It was a winter's night when love first met us
Frosted was the land, the sky sparkled with
Many stars. The cold was kept at bay by the
Warmth of passion.

Walking hand-in-hand, we stopped beneath the
Hawthorn tree, the stars twinkled in your
Eyes. My heart raced upon our embrace, we
Were lovers' silhouette by the moonlight.

Our sense of togetherness was unequalled
In the universe we fused as one, your kiss
Was electric, the greatest pleasure to
Behold me.

Our caressing was Utopia, we floated in
Celestial splendour, whispers we shared
Of thoughts rhythmically entwined, locked
By the emotions of love.

Duncan MacFarlane

A Bereavement

When you go through a bereavement
A divorce or a death
Or that feeling where you're
At a complete loss
You go through bewilderment
Confusion and pain
Knowing you will never see
That person again
It takes a long time
To overcome your fears
That person isn't there
To wipe away your tears
You are lost without them
You become a recluse
Don't go out just read the news
Everything you do
Is like starting again
Don't know when you'll feel better
There's no way of knowing
You just keep your chin up
Put on a brave face
You find the strength
To just keep going
You get depressed
And feel really low
You just put on a show
But deep down your emotions
Are shattered and torn
You get that feeling
You wish you weren't born
But keep going
You'll get stronger every day
Keep your chin up
Other things will come your way.

Ellen Rowley

SNOW FALLS

I see, snow clinging to pine branches
Watching them fall, one by one unto the ground
Stealing the sounds of wind-swept leaves
As to fool us, that they're not around.

James Patrick Milton

OUR TREASURE

'Twas many days ago since you were last seen,
I imagine the sight I once knew so well,
And look under the stars where forever it's been
Our love, only love, that pricelessly sells.

Through windows so clear does your face not show,
Open and vibrant in the sun did shine,
Now blocked, still blocked within layers of snow,
Left cheerful to know once the windows were thine.

But no matter what hinders, we are eternal.
Our love is the ocean, endless indeed.
Despite she, she whose traits so maternal,
Struggling I served when she was in need.

The miles keep us apart thwart you to endeavour
Through love, our love I shall not see thee ever.

James T Gordon

Unknown Universe

They are long halls that I look down,
turning away from the now and facing the then.
A faint light is visible at the end,
always casting dusty rays towards me.

On either side are doors
and open spaces where I can be.
On the soft or hard floors,
I meet up with faces and places of an earlier reality.

I don't always know what is behind each,
it may be a room of colour, music, or laughter,
sadness, compassion or indifference.
Sometimes it is love,
depending on which,
I have a different experience.

I don't always choose which direction I take,
often I find myself floating along,
drifting on a gentle current
of which I cannot decipher the point.
And I am merely traversing the rivulets
and blind caverns of my mind.
I move along the corridors afloat,
always a few inches off the ground.

I never reach the end where the light
steadily burns,
though it is a gentle flame, that basks and warms my face.
I am wary, as perhaps this would be the room
in which I might want to lock the key
behind me, never to return.

Gina M Clayton

THE VENDOR

Who will buy my wonderful poems
Who will buy one from me today
Who will ready my wonderful lyrics
Who will sing as they go on their way
Who will buy my wonderful poems
Who will help keep the wolves from the door
Who will stop for a while and listen?
Buy a story from me - today.

Opal Innsbruk

Who Makes Snowflakes?

Who makes snowflakes,
Is it God above?
Entwined with angel love,
Each one has a face,
Each one a time in space,
A filigree of lace,
Fall to earth
And disappear without trace.
Are they the angels' tears
The clouds have been saving up for years?
Frozen frost,
A snowman who's got lost,
As an icicle appears,
Are they made by a snow machine,
With a peppermint-coated sheen?
But I can only dream
Of who makes snowflakes.

Alan Pow

EARTH TO EARTH

From Earth we rise
To gain our place,
They hear our cries -
They see our face.
We feel, we want,
We need, we see.
Soft voices calm our fears.
We hear and touch,
We want to be,
Loved so very dear.

We bring forth siblings,
Spread our seeds.
In every walk of life.
Our Lord is watching over -
Husbands, sons, their wives.
We build a world
To mould our needs,
From rags to riches
We succeed.
We plant and sow,
To reap rewards,
All nature grows,
We thank our Lord.

Our lambs are warm,
The cattle sweet,
We grow the corn
That we may eat.
We love, we live,
We go our course,
From hence we rose
Back to: the Earth.

Wendy Watkin

AN AFTERNOON PARTY

All the ladies are retired
They get together and raise a smile
Sitting in the lounge together
Seems to give them a lot of pleasure

Talk and knitting is the theme
To keep up with what has been
Happening from week to week
You cannot drop off to sleep

Joan had crocheted a hat and slippers
Annette found they did not fit her
Peg and Doris tried on the hat
Saying, 'What do you think of that?'

Peg brought some wool today
Because she did not want to throw it away
The wool was all in skeins
It really did puzzle Doris and Elsie's brains

Not one end but two they found
In this muddled up skein
The ladies were laughing fit to bust
It really did amuse the rest of us

How the balls got tangled up
But those two ladies did not give up
Until that skein of wool was done
Even while Doris sang she carried on

It is great to see these ladies enjoy themselves
Bringing back stories of the past
Singing songs and knitting away
On their very special day.

J Bradbury

PAINTING PICTURES

Paint me a picture, here in my mind,
Of nature's beauty when the summer sun shines.
Of breathtaking scenery, the view from a hill,
The clear tumbling water, past the old water mill.

Views from the cliff tops, across sparkling seas,
The flowers in my garden, and pollen-coated bees,
A golden sandy beach with rocks and pools,
Young children playing at the little village school.

The bluebells in the woods, the sun filtering through,
Young cows in their fields, as they lazily chew,
Those beautiful clouds, the magnificent trees,
There are so many things that I still long to see.

I can hear birds singing, I can smell the cut grass,
Please leave me those senses, that's all that I ask.
I remember nature's gifts here in my mind,
But oh how I miss them, now that I'm blind.

Dennis Young

ON YOU I DEPEND

My Jesus, on you I depend.
I'll trust you right through to the end.
Through good times or bad, when happy or sad,
I'll lean on your power, and know every hour,
That you are my saviour and friend.

Whatever the future may bring,
To my faith in Jesus I'll cling.
In sickness or health, in need or in wealth,
I'll trust in the love you send from above,
And know you're my saviour and friend.

When heartaches and sorrows abide,
I know you are there by my side.
Though dark is the way, and weary the day,
My pathway is clear, your spirit is near,
When I know my saviour and friend.

Margaret Cameron

A Stranger In Line

Standing in tranquil stillness
There was a touch of sadness
Within his eyes and stature
Not for himself, yet, for us
We stood in steel cold rows
Awaiting the stern, 'Next.'
Breadline, the stranger to dignity
Those who serve are tired
And long to be somewhere else
In a warm bed, but duty calls
Nameless, faceless we pass
Before them, amongst them
Equal under God, not in this line.
For those who give, have power
We have hunger, and want
Vulnerable, frozen fingers, take only
The blessed gift of giving stolen
yet, the stranger in the line
Brings dignity, a oneness.
In the silences of his being
The pain of rejection
Written on his face, his eyes
Search the heart and touch the soul
There is an amazing kindness
In the grace of his being.
'Next', and we all shuffle forward
I watch the man as he breaks bread
He comes amongst us
Sharing the little he has
In the light of dignity
He holds us, for a moment one
As we share his meal
And somehow we feel
Restored, whole, a person
Light of light in our darkest day

We, the unworthy, the rejected
Graced by the stranger
Amongst us, within us
On the breadline.

A R Wait

CHRISTMAS

C arols sung from the heart,
H ear the angels shake their wings:
R aise your heads as children pray.
I wish the world peace and joy
S ounds of bells that ring in peace.
T he Saviour came and joy was felt:
M ay you see the love that's given,
A special prayer may be given,
S ing within this peace given.

R Mills

REALITY

Reality,
What is it?
Is it love with you?
Or being alone?
Is it marriage?
Growing old together?
Or is it being on your own?

Reality,
I'd like to know
What it is?
Whether it's happiness,
Or whether it's sadness.
Is it love?
Being with you?
Or is it being on your own?

Reality,
I wonder if I'll ever know?
Whether it's with you?
Or without you?
Whether we'll get married?
Or whether we'll be on our own?

S Longford

WHOSE HONOUR?

Many a title, too many a one
For reasons special in a way
A tribute of achievements
Not more than a passing show.

A name of famousness
A heavy burden to become,
It lingers like an odour
For those who follow its perfume.

Christ they crucified
For being the greatest one,
An example in humbleness
For us to follow on and on.

To honour his sacrifice
In meek and willing ways
Asking blessings for all
Good, the power to pray
Is in each willing one.

A privilege to all mankind
From God, to honour
In faithfulness
The glory comes not by chance
Or earthly deed, or without
'A sacrifice of human nature'
That is.

Rachel Taylor

LIKE WHAT YOU SEE

Your eyes look straight down into the depths of the real me.
You see *me*.
There's no hiding,
I like being exposed to you.

My head is high as I walk down the street,
Proud to be yours,
Proud to say you're mine.

I wake up and you're watching me -
Watching me dreaming.
You touch my face and smile at me,
All I can do is kiss you.

You undress my emotions until there is only me.
And you like what you see.

Kara Sian Phillips

THE REFUGEE

Sorry you've no friend now lady,
striding staunch our shattered streets,
infant son bewildered, staring
stark through dark and haunted eyes.

Sorry it's no haven here,
and hoodlums wage a senseless war
on those in Eastern cloth,
rejecting the rich counterpoint of foreign tongue.

Sorry that the artist lied
with honeyed words to tempt the young,
made sequinned song to store his gold
from anarchy of selfishness,
not protest born of care.

Sorry you're an eyesore
to the rich and pampered toys.
Their world is closed (as always)
to actions born from fear
and impulse of despair.

Anne Gaelan

THE SHADOW

It follows me around,
Wherever I go,
I can't escape,
As it will know.

Maybe one day,
I can chase it away,
If I can only find,
The words to say.

I don't want to be
Surrounded by night,
Gripping my throat,
So, so tight.

Take it away,
And let there be light,
Let's chase this shadow
Into the night.

Alan Gordon

SYMPATHY

Be honest with yourself
Don't leave space
For repeating
Once living memories
Used to replace
Any love that's fleeting
Alter a season's misery
To a summer of beautiful joy
Throw away emotions of bitterness
To happiness found to be pure
We all feel periods of sympathy
We all have tears to cry
Gain strength from possessions
And the loved ones at your side.

Paul Fulton

AND SO COLD WINTER

And so cold winter.
No more garden summer's warmth,
Long wine glass evenings,
Smooth skin body-damp nights
Snatched away by ice-hearted
Year's-end darkness.
The back door suddenly sharp shut
On hot snatched kisses
And so cold winter
Hanging onto the bitter
Fading, weak light, enough to still
Peer through anger's mist to see the
start in searing sunglass glare
Bare feet on heat-starched seafront
Sweat-streaked dance,
Tasting sizzling sugar lips that
Stopped the world, just two lovers
Hot moist bodies entwined
And so cold winter
Whose wickedly slick rain
Suddenly poured and
Washed the summer's love away
And so cold winter
Lay your frost, ice my longing
It will endure the longest nights, for I am
Waiting for summer's searing heat
To dry my tears . . .

David Elsmere

PERPETUAL

Contemplation deep into
The blackness before me,
The river so calm
I will to be in its solemnity

Blinding light breaks right
False promises don't fool,
The impending grey skies
Are reflecting my soul.

The grey skies they open,
Rain down, sorrow real.
Shrouded it hears me,
Lachrymology ethereal.

This emptiness so deep,
A river so inviting,
Searching for answers,
Resisting not enlightening.

Continuing, I yearn
To live again true,
One prevailing desire
To give my heart to you.

River mirror my life,
This perpetual misery.
One day I want to say,
This is all a fallacy.

Adam J Tipper

WHITE COPPICE

Oh wondrous, thundering gorge,
How oft' have I been in your hidden places,
Felt your walls squeezing me as I forge
Through your rapidly rising river bases.
Then violently, peat-stained fluids spill
Crashing down the crevice so far.
You rest, from this race down the hill.
Breath caught, flow slowly to the reservoir.
I scramble the narrow sheep trail, and fight
Grasses growing like hairs around your pit,
Only to emerge at vertiginous height
And stare at your tree-crowned summit,
To wonder at the pilots' monument so
Then to descend to the batsman's field below.

Leslie Russell Walker

Not Lonely, But Alone

Many people floating around,
Me in the middle,
None of them touch me,
None of them reach me,
Pulled one way,
Pushed another, but
Nothing touches me,
Nothing reaches me,
Talking, chattering,
Wanting, needing, but
None of them touch me,
None of them reach me,
Places to go,
Things to be done, but
Nothing touches me,
Nothing reaches me,
Never lonely, but
Always alone.

Gillian L Wise

EMBERS

His once steaming mug is empty now
But still he craves more to warm him
Over the embers he could see the city lights
Flickering against the darkness beyond

While the night sky formed a sequinned backdrop
With the odd wispy cloud staining its glittering countenance
The chatter of wheel over points in the yard beyond
Broke the cold, wintry silence of the night

The night express then lifts the wind; hurrying south
Windows flashing, but no smiles, just empty seats
going where, and for what purpose?
Other than to stir the embers as it hurtles by.

Placing the kettle on the trivet over the glowing coals
He turns and waves to an expectant face in the signal box
No greeting returned, only a metallic click behind him
As the points on the down line reflect an unseen action from within

Duty done, he sits waiting for the steam to rise once more
Switching on his radio he searches for the soft strains
That will warm him, with his brew
Something soft and mellow, with words to match his mood

Finding what he wanted, he reaches out and stirs the embers
He loads more coke onto the warming brazier below the kettle
Now steaming gently into the dark, then filling his mug
He leans back smiling, relaxed and content with his lot.

John Osland

THE LITTLE ANGEL

There was a little angel
Who sat upon a cloud
To play her harp she loved to do
But always much too loud.
She was called into the office
By Him who sits above
And told if it continued she would be
Keeper of the doves.
Now this it was a punishment
Or it was meant to be,
But Little Angel sat above and
Clapped her hands with glee.
She talked to Father Gabriel
To ask what she should do.
Should she go on playing loudly,
The answer came, 'Oh no!
Play quietly Little Angel,
And if you're very good,
I will take you down a rainbow
to play in an earthly wood.'

Now Little Angel thought and thought
And came to this conclusion,
If she went down to Earth again,
It would only cause confusion.
So if you hear a heavenly harp
Playing loudly up above,
Do not despair, it's only her
Making merry with the doves.

Elizabeth Marsden

Tears

Tears filling my eyes
as I think of you.
My furry, cuddly, faithful cat.

I remember so well your kitten days,
playing with feathers,
chasing a ball upstairs and down,
enjoying the garden . . .

I remember your mature years,
loving to sit out in the sun,
peeping out from next door's hedge,
chasing back indoors to eat.

I look at you now . . .
sleeping by the fire,
knowing you have cancer
and will one day leave me.

It breaks my heart into tears.

Mags Scorey

TESTIMONY!

Looking through my mind's eye I see myself in a different light
A mental picture I just can't adhere to like a mirror showing my life
in plight
This place I have lived all my life buried deep down inside me
Turning and teasing, shouting and screaming, the light I need to see

I could become this person, true changes it will take however
Though not unreachable like anything in life
Thought provoking, inspirational and clever
And as I change and grow a rule I must endeavour to show
In a system I'm involved in a place I wish not go or stay
I'll search long and hard however to change my life today

I'm not educated highly enough, I let myself right down
So I'll have to take another approach, I've had my chances it's true
Messed it up and made others frown but hey, that's what I do
As deep down I know and feel I was born into a decent family
Into a decent place, the problems however, lie upon the world's surface
My destiny I know is my own and that is what I'll chase

Nothing better to do anyway and hey, I could even save some face
Not pushing it back at people who have tried to put me in my place
but offering thanks for their criticism, it helped me off the fence
That will give me great satisfaction to show others and also it just
makes sense

Begging forgiveness from my saviour and a wish to be transported
As this part of earth I live simply makes me feel distorted
Happier being I am no doubt, but all this has to be reported
Fresh from my mind's eye then written down and then retorted

Look around, look at the unhappy stranger's face, something inside
                                              me used to burn
Telling it was not real, if this is life how we should be living then
                                              from ourselves we steal
Thankfully he came and saved me from the hatred in the world,
                                                      I'm overawed
For this of course I'm eternally grateful and in this poem I hereby
                                                  praise the Lord.

Matt Riley

SAFE AND SECURE

You feel secure when top of the class,
and when your priest is preaching mass.
Or when a coal fire warms aching flesh,
and siblings slumber in their crèche.

You feel secure in a nuclear shelter,
and at the bottom of a helter-skelter.
Or when you click a seat-belt on,
and when you detect a magician's con.

You feel secure with a peaceful death,
and when soothed by a lover's breath.

J Watcher-Masters

MATTHEW

When I look at you my child of pain,
I see myself under your lovely skin,
The fear, the loss and loneliness again.
I want to help your deeper cry,
And soothe your brow with love and care,
And free your soul before you die.
Your silent tear left me a broken man,
It showed me something deep inside,
A child that hides; that always ran.
When I see you, I feel so much,
I understand the fear that hides away,
That's needs to be seen for a loving touch.
Maybe we can help each other,
And walk the path, hand in hand, heart to heart,
To face the fear and look within, to find our friend.
Words could never explain our tears,
They search around and lose their way,
It's only our hearts that have the skill, to look and dare.
Forgive me son for leaving you, to fend alone,
I was lost myself from a life pain,
From my father who had a heart of stone.

Ricky N Lock

ONE TRUE FRIEND

What joy, what happiness
Being with you
My one true friend
So kind, so true.

What joy, what happiness
With just us two
My one true friend
How I love you.

Marian Bythell

A Messily Starred Sky

Jami, sudden rain last night awoke me.
In heart, perhaps something closed,
You may have told me. Your rage, pain,
I guessed . . . what kept away from me.
You, anymore, just don't come!

Jami, a messily starred sky saddens,
Your shadowed hand, stunned eye,
Our glimpse at Venus and Mars,
Mercury, Jupiter, a quite rebellious Uranus.
O believe me, I kept those pilgrimages
Ever-imaginary fresh!

Jami, just to wish on your birthday
Tomorrow before the day begins -
Will pick few flowers from the tub, I
Will play our favourite tune!

Shuvra Rahman

O Muse, Ordain That I Should Sing

O Muse, ordain that I should sing
Your praises by your font today;
Betake in burdened arms to bring
Morn's freshly blossomed blooms of May.
To sing as thou doth wont to sing
To fairer beings on shores of Blest;
Proffer to pour, and set on wing,
Undying cadence of endless zest!
That Posterity grants a place
Amongst minstrels of agéd fame,
Who by your font once drank your grace,
To immortalise fair their name!

Malcolm Henry James

SELF-MADE MAN

Self-made man, what a shark
Dirty deals done in the dark

Chasing money all the time
Don't you think it's such a crime?

Blood pressure up, stress level high
In a few years you can say goodbye
That ain't a word of a lie

Greedy, bloated, slavery chops
You'll never make the top of the pops

Social standing to admire
Don't mess with me, 'cause your playing with fire

On and up the slippery pole, you should be put back on the dole
That's possibly your best role

Treading on toes on the way up
I don't wish you the best of luck

Directorships here, family there
You and your son make a right pair

Have a good send off, give your worldly goods away
At your funeral nobody will pray.

Brian Lunt

YOU'RE NOT QUALIFIED TO SAY THAT

I am merely a mortal soul and I cannot live a thousand years;
These are the words that sub-consciously slide into our ears;
These are the words of today's society,
We're here and now we lack variety.
Who dares stand before me and tell me I *have not* lived before,
A plight of a false world I cannot ignore.
For our future we must open the spiritual door,
The door that has no key, for it has never been locked.
But until now we never knew how to open it, we merely knocked;
No one can tell me that I am wrong, that I sing the words to a
                                                              forbidden song.
A qualification is a good temptation, but don't let social status
                                                               corrupt a nation;
Status is nothingness, a form of control; we're self-obsessed,
                                                      we're losing our soul.
People! Open your eyes, feel the ground and look up to the skies.

Louise Tucker

THE LOVER'S REAL ANSWER

'This is a real lovers' question,'
he said and then asked,
'But why?'
'Because you trust me,'
she said,
'and because I cry.'
'Why?'
'Because you breathe in my breath,'
she said with a sigh.
'But why?' he said.
She took his head
and turned it to the sky.
'Look,' she said,
'that's where angels fly.'
'But why?' he insisted.
'Because God decided,'
she persisted.
'But why do you love me?' he demanded.
'Because God commanded
that's why.'

AnnMarie Eldon

ABOUT RUGBY

It was Saturday, 22nd November, 2003
In the inclement weather of Sydney, Australia.
England were in the final of the rugby World Cup.
The whole nation was excited at the news,
Everyone praying it would not be another sporting blues.
The stage was set, England v Australia
As hysteria hit the world of rugby mania.
A game where the first five points,
Went to Australia.
England dug in determined to do their thing.
After a much even-stevens game,
At fourteens, England struck bold.
Making it seventeen-seventeen
At the time all told.
With minutes to go,
The Aussies struck gold.
Seventeen - seventeen
Onward extra time rolled.
With a minute left,
An England drop goal
From Jonny Wilkinson,
Our number one goal scorer,
And to the proud nation's delight
The reigning champions fold.
Ending the match in the rain and the cold
The new reigning champions,
Will be of an English mould
And the rugby World Cup was ours to hold.
A sweet chariot carried it home,
Then paraded it around the streets of London,
Telling the emphatic ode.

Ali Sebastian

The Mystic

Mystic, shifty-footed, blinkered half-eye,
Sanguine, softly peers, peerlessly at
All, and breathes forth wispy meanings;
The inartistic, graceless eloquence
Teasing the ignorant and unwise
Who bow their heads before the draft
Of not-knowledge impressively proclaimed.

Colin Walsh

Avatar

I see the sun as she smiles down on me,
Bestowing her power into my mortal vessel.
This brilliant light, pure,
An aura of incomprehensible delight.
I am favoured by the elements.

These hands were once frail, weak,
Are now sources of radiating joy. How can this be?
I am only a servant of the higher elementals.
This divination, is it merely a hallucination?
No . . . I am the chosen one.
My purpose is clear.

My soul is free from these mortal bounds
The energy of Gaia, the energy of me,
Everywhere; for I am everything.
I control the wind, the ocean answers to me,
Yet I am nothing.

My ascension to this throne, merely an illusion
Created by powers, higher than the stars?
This cannot be. I am supreme, above all others
I am not a pawn in this twisted reality
I refuse to play this game.

The heavens have cast me out; falling from rapture.
I plead with Pluto to restore my power,
Echoing through fragments of time,
Chaos in my wake, destroying all I hold dear.
Once again I am fragile.

David Randall

STAIRCASE

Climbing twelve
steps of the wooden
staircase, my tiny
feet moved from one
step to the next
as I held jutting
timber, protecting
me from tumbling
back to the cement
floor of our home.
When I was older,
scrubbing the stairs
loosened pieces
of grain that stuck
into my fingernails,
hurting my skin.
A smell of rawness
filled my nostrils
while I worked my
way down each step.
From flowing water,
the cold floor wet
I'd mop it up with
an old rag and cover
the ground with well-
read newspapers until
it dried, the bucket
of dirty water flung
weekly into a hole at
the end of our street.

Mary Guckian

THE JOB SEEKER'S ALLOWANCE

It was like an itch
you couldn't scratch,
a torso you
couldn't dispose of
      till it got
to the stage
there were that many
undead corpses
left lying around that
his decomposing family
didn't know which
way to turn to escape
their limbless insurrection.

The limbs were what he
wanted to do with his life;
chop them off and call them
attempted occupations.

But the torsos lingered on -
unsettling and in the way
of real progress, actual
accomplishment.

Eventually no one
believed his alibis.
If he wasn't in one job,
chopping it off, he'd
be at another making excuses.
All his disembodied family
could do was
wait for Daddy to come home.

Peter Asher

DECISIONS, DECISIONS, DECISIONS

And so 2004 marks my last year at school,
Only A-levels await, the final duel.
Having spent the last seven years at the same institution,
The thought of now leaving spreads anxiety and confusion.
It seems as though there are three options open to me,
But what the new year brings, we shall have to wait and see.

Perhaps the most common route is university or college,
An extension of school, to acquire more knowledge,
But with Open Days and interviews,
Offers and prospectuses to peruse,
The decision of whether to stay at home,
Or move into Halls and go it alone,
Assignments, essays and paying the tuition fee,
There is so much to consider to obtain a degree.

Seeking employment is the second possibility,
One which I greet with some hostility,
For the thought of a full-time job does not fill me with glee,
Before working 'nine to five', I want to be free.
The idea of documents and contracts being created
Does not sound as though I would be liberated.

The third and final choice, I shall consider here,
It is of course opting for a gap year.
The thought of discovering new countries does sound appealing,
Exploring cultures and landmarks would be revealing,
Also reserving a year for travel
Would give me some more time to unravel
The next step I want to take and what I want to achieve,
Something which at present seems difficult to conceive.

I do not want to sound as though I am complaining,
For I am fortunate to have choices that are not constraining,
It's just that whatever I decide after my exams in June,
I feel the decision will have to be made all too soon!

Ruth Morris

SUBCONSCIOUS WINTER

I love the winter like I love my mother
Winter, winter, winter, at last
Time to breathe, release the demons of the past
Winter, winter, cold and crisp
Suspended life, an absolute calm
Those beautiful vivid grey skies
Just can't describe my feelings
It's as though winter makes me stand still
And brings on a strange kind of melancholy
To touch the ice, the cool air all around me
And in the distance the crows crowing
Their winter song.

Terry Lane

THE HONESTY OF YOU

It's a struggle of emotions with feelings of pain
It is a message from mind to soul, saying things will never be the same.
There is a conflict within that others cannot see,
And you know no matter how you try, you can never be free

Of the cruel circumstance that ordained you should live
With such internal pain, how could you ever forgive,
The reasons behind this emotional state,
Which ultimately can only be put down to fate.

But the spirit within you reaches out to take hold,
Of life and a future, that enables feelings to unfold.
So even if the reasons for your pain and despair
Are in the background, and will always be there.

You still have the capacity to give love and receive,
And the strength to try to understand the ones who deceive.
Because there are those in your life, who are loyal and true,
And they know the soul, and the honesty of you.

B Lamus

ROMNEY VALE

Down where the sea meets the sky, where the clouds hover, where the old chapel stands like a lonely sentinel, a young mother pushed her pram.

It was January and summer was far away, and the wind blew down along Hythe seafront, the waves crashed onto the shore.

The child in the pram began to cry - loud noises. 'She cries loud,' said a lone bystander, and all the while, the clouds hovered.

Somebody was playing Schubert in their bedroom - as the rising tones replaced the low ones. Up on the nearby hills, snow was falling, and 'neath the shining, round, white moon, frost was glistening.

Along the seashore, people were fishing, and ever the clouds did hover, till darkness fell. And the baby cried, 'Oh, oh, oh,'

Peter Alfred Buss

THE RAIN

Come down, the rain
We are in the garden without a fruit
At the gate, we stood
With prayer of blissful moment
And imagination of the blue sky

Where is the rain?
Situation is tough
Come and topple the dry,
The greens to replace the browns
With pain of time
The rain,
Shower to heal the pains
The bones are tired
And knees are injured
But we beg the rain
To pardon the imperfection

We are odd
But claiming we are right
The rain of peace to chase our odds
For the pain is much

We beckoned the evil
And conjured the rain
From its sting emerged the gain
Within the neighbour
We lost the love
And the rain ceased to fall

We caught the snow with odds
But never sufficient
We beg the rain
To save the world from distress.

Ojo Idowu Opeyemi

Your Poem Mum

I love you very much Mum,
And hate to see you cry.
I hope this poem cheers you up,
And this is not a lie.
I love it when you smile, Mum,
It brightens up my day.
I hate it when I see you cry,
That blows my light away.
So Mummy please cheer up,
It would really make my day,
It would bring the light right back to me
And never fade away.

Abbie S Dixon

SWEET-SMELLING AND WARM

It's sweet-smelling and warm and a comfort inside,
with my life as it is I feel on a high.

It's hard to describe like a sudden dry thirst,
however relaxed I want to just burst.

I haven't always felt this secure deep in me,
my eyes have now opened and I can clearly see,

Because life isn't always a drama and stress,
for recently I'm able to reassess less.

I think it was New Year when I turned over my leaf,
for now I feel a strong hand holding beneath.

The pressure has lifted; the sweet songs are being sung,
my life has direction, thank God for the breath in my lungs.

For God is my power and His work will be done,
through me and through you and through everyone.

I feel I can conquer for I am the best,
it's been added to my life, my cupful of zest.

By my side stand strong, my family and friends,
for generations to come, life will never end.

So this new lease of life, sweet-smelling and warm
was a comfort inside since the day I was born.

Steven Howe

A Mother's Prayer

Wouldn't it be nice
if things were sold at a really low price?

Wouldn't it be nice
if people wouldn't stand and stare?

Wouldn't it be nice
if my child combed her hair?

Wouldn't it be nice
if there was no rock 'n' roll?

Wouldn't it be nice
if we still had control?

Wouldn't it be nice
if they didn't make a mess?

Wouldn't it be nice
if they caused me less stress?

Wouldn't it be nice
if all these things came true?

Wouldn't it be nice
if I had one less of you?

Lillian Hutt (12)

A Hole In The Clouds

love is irresistible
to love we are drawn
love is what we are
to love we are born

my birth was from sunshine
shone on me a ray
an eternal child
in the dirt i play

digging deep for diamonds
platinum abundant
all that glitters is my gold
stones and mud redundant

i paint a picture in my mind
luminous and sparkling
electric connection
to the earth is arcing

tingling with ecstasy
delighting in dizziness
home at last, back to the past
realm of light's open for business

Mark Musgrave

THE ONLY DANCE

Life is the last waltz
Steps forward
        Steps sideways
Steps backwards
        Circles made
This is the final dance
        So play your tune
Be still the winter long
        And prepare
Then fiddle out the music
Of your heart and through June
Please my ear when the roses bloom
And dry my tears when the petals fall
Let our breathing mix
With the early morning dew
And let me climb the hill
Where each step brings me nearer
        And nearer to you
Let me take my chance
        Teach me how to dance.

Clive Cornwall

THE OLDER MAN

Varieties of love are like varieties of cereal.
Some you become addicted to,
some make you nauseous in the morning.
Well, this one's new to me, it's made of a different material.
Quite a sneaky thing, it crept up on me without any warning.
You see he's a grown-up, a man, much older than me,
and he's got a girlfriend, but he says he's not in love.
But he's lying, he loves her, it's plain to see,
so there's no chance of him giving her the shove.
In fact, next week he's taking her to Milan,
and he keeps going on about how excited he is
but I just want him to take me, take my hand,
because only I understand how precious this man is.

M C F McKinlay

SAFE

When you die, you go out of fashion
In the sort of photographs they don't make anymore.
People will laugh at your hairstyle.
You will be seen, as if through the wrong end of a telescope,
Bracketed by start and finish years,
Like the walls of a remote and strange hotel room
That has no phone or return address.

People are breezes that stir paper on desks
And scatter trinkets. They leave behind
Things that seem more solid than themselves:
A penknife with the name of a lager on the handle,
An expired season ticket, some shoes.

Scientists say life's all the position of the observer.
They say near to, someone seems dead but - far away -
Maybe on another planet, through a powerful telescope,
You can see them still alive, safe for ever in 1970,
Like a plastic rocket in a cereal bowl.

But if you talk to them,
You still have to imagine their answer.

Michael Brett

DAYDREAMS

Sitting and resting so it seems . . .
Nothing doing but having daydreams . .
One moment I close my eyes so tight . .
Next minute that *dream* is out of sight . .
Daydreaming's my favourite thing to do . .
Come rain or shine . . . how about you?

Carol Olson

LOVELY GRAN
(To Mam, with fondest memroes of your dearest departed mother, Gran)

- You are indeed most personally delightful,
With all of your ladylike elegance,
You marvellously grace
The very scene itself
Wherever and whenever you go.

- For your absolutely angelic posture
Does, without doubt,
Seriously enhance
The very purpose of daily life itself.

- Your sublimely personal attributes
Do unquestionably magnify
The complete essence of
Your distinctly unique persona
Both for now and for all time.

- With your most innately supreme presence
To surround us consistently along
With your undeniably wonderful charisma,
These special gifts
Can and do,
With full thoughtfulness,
No wrong at all.

- So your totally undivided magnetism,
In itself,
Can only notably exemplify
Your whole individual worth
To each of us.

- From now straight through until
The inevitable conclusion of
The entire goodness
Which is deeply rooted
Within your very being itself.

Michael Stalker

ABSENT MIND

The new toothbrush bends
like a bushman's saw blade
the bristles are short and soft
and worth every penny of fourteen pence.

I chide myself at my utter penny-pinching
and yet I suppose that is me.

I also purchase a small black comb
measuring four inches by one inch,
costing forty-five pence.
That being two pence a tooth
and yet again I suppose that is me.

My brain feels dull, my hair
lifeless and hoary.
Brylcreem. Ah yes
I've left that at home
along with the comb, toothbrush,
slippers and one or two other things.

The only items I had to remember,
I had forgotten.
But what's in a memory after the event . . .
Absolution!

Thomas Allan Liddle

Fireworks

Secure in Hampshire enclave
'midst clustered pine trees
we played 'big bangs',
learning the dangerous game.

High explosives, gun-cotton primers,
fast fuses, booby traps,
grenades and mines,
amotal and demolition skills.

This was not Guy Fawkes,
nor Bonfire Night and sparklers;
nor yet Roman candles and squibs,
Though thunderflashes played their part.

Hair-raising to touch a mine,
or light a sensitive fuse,
finger-plugging one's ears
against explosion pressure.

Daring briefly to look
as whole structures seemed to melt
into dusty clouds
and rubble heap.

How good to go on leave, and
meet that girl at the bonfire,
when friendship turned to love
and sparklers on her finger.

Jo Allen

RACISM

What is racism?
Oh, I can't pronounce it well
Do you know, what is that?

Do you know? We're all the same,
Black, white and brown,
'Please, please oh God of people
You forget this wrong way.'

Do you know we have a God,
Christian and Muslim,
But I have one thought,
You can believe in that
What your heart wants.

Please, we must forget
The word 'racism'.

Zyfe Cani

When The Darkness Comes

Silence pounds inside my head
And deafens me to reason,
Dark depression grips, it squeezes,
Numbs my struggling thoughts

Then swimming through a sea
Of suffocating boredom,
I submit to an endless reality
Which my life so distorts.

Kim Montia

FOLLOW THE SUN

Nobody can bridge our spirits
The strength of our resolve will attest to all rights.

Banished visionaries amid the lost dreams,
Walk along a new path
Seeking the current past
Looking for fulfilment.
Eyes twinkle skywards
Like beacons in the desert
The idealistic a symbol of
The grail of serenity.

The versifiers spellbound
By the enigma of art.
The utterances of the mystics
Lost in the Elysium Fields,
Searching for the symbols
That cross the boundaries of time.
Antediluvian prophets watch
And listen to our wishes,
Try to direct us
Through the never-ending blue.

I have glimpsed the fervour
In the hearts of lovers,
Breathing in the images
Inside the intensity of their credence.
Hate obliterates the essence
Of those who strive to preach it.
I will glide in the fantasies
That they cry with such tenderness.

Bathed in the purity of the sun's light
Shattered illusions are brought back from the dead.

Vicky Stevens

The Great Eye

Why do you summon me, great eye, what is it?
I see a terrible impending doom, on the blue planet!
And you must go there to stop it.
What doom? Great eye, please do impart.
Atomic tomfoolery, that's what I see!
Inflamed, uncontrollable fingers, flicking out.
Insane eyes, darting, to and fro, to and fro.
Go now and neutralise every single mind,
Of those with fidgety, flickering fingers.
We must not allow the most beautiful orb,
In the universe to be destroyed.
Scorched, blackened, beyond recognition,
The great eye never lies!

If I take away the mind of those, with fidgety, flickering fingers,
There will be chaos and no one to lead the masses.
They will recover soon enough, and have done so before.
Hopefully, good men, with clean minds, will prevail.
Full of pure logic.
Go! Go now, before it is too late,
You have so little time.

Terry Ramanouski

THE SKINNIEST TO WIN

She is trapped.
There's no way out.
What she eats,
Is all she thinks about.
She's so preoccupied,
With how her body looks.
Forever counting calories,
In those little *calorie* books.
I've been telling her for months now,
That she really isn't fat.
I keep telling her she's gorgeous,
But she won't believe any of that.
I've tried to get it through to her,
All that matters is what's inside.
Even after the slightest weight gain,
I have to comfort her while she cries.
She's actually pretty clever,
She knows every trick in the book.
From how to miss out on meals,
To making herself puke.
She once went without eating,
For nearly a whole week.
To try and gain the superwaif image,
Bony, slender, sleek.
It's killing me with worry,
What she's putting herself through.
She's not only destroying her body,
But her character and personality too.
I think she's getting skinnier,
She must weigh less than six stone.
She can no longer live with her family,
She now exists in a hospital room, all alone.

I saw her mum the other day,
She couldn't take the strain anymore.
'The whole family's distraught,' she said,
'What's my daughter doing this for?'
Her face is drawn and skeletal,
She is drained of all strength to fight.
Her rib cage is completely visible,
A total wreck, what a frail sight.
There is nothing more, the doctors can do,
She's sixteen, too old to be force fed.
What a waste of a young girl's life,
My greatest fear is that she'll end up dead.

Donna Whalley

Munching Maggot

I hear it writhing like a munching maggot,
In its rotting cheese,
Dug deep in its mouldy wormhole,
Of vice and sleaze.

That dirty tramp,
In the expensive attire,
Has me full of loathing
And spitting ferocious fire.

I hope we don't meet,
Or fists will fly.
I will aim high
And poke it in the eye.

I hate its vicious voice,
Its motivation is so plain.
It's all out war,
As I hear it munching again.

I'll whip it with words,
If it wriggles my way.
So much to it,
I would have to say.

Carol Ann Darling

People Of Third World

People of Third World are there to be crushed
People of these nations are living in their own prisons
A child dies of hunger with his dreams left to linger
People of Third World are there to be crushed
They say there is peace and harmony in a world full of irony
People of Third World are there to be crushed
They look at the sky for the help to come by
When the help comes by it comes without a smile
People of Third World are there to be crushed
Their hope is dying and belief is flying
People of Third World are there to be crushed
Their dreams are dying and the time is flying
People of Third World are there to be crushed
Hope a day comes with a world full of welcomes
People of Third World are there to be crushed
These are the words of a person
Who wants a world without assumptions
People of Third World are there to be crushed.

Ibrahim Asad

SUBMISSIONS INVITED
SOMETHING FOR EVERYONE

POETRY NOW 2004 - Any subject, any style, any time.

WOMENSWORDS 2004 - Strictly women, have your say the female way!

STRONGWORDS 2004 - Warning! Opinionated and have strong views. (Not for the faint-hearted)

All poems no longer than 30 lines.
Always welcome! No fee!
Cash Prizes to be won!

Mark your envelope (eg *Poetry Now*) **2004**
Send to:
Forward Press Ltd
Remus House, Coltsfoot Drive,
Peterborough, PE2 9JX

**OVER £10,000 POETRY PRIZES
TO BE WON!**

Judging will take place in October 2004